Superior Coaches
- *The Bowen Story* -
A Pictorial History Of The Bowen Coach Group

Superior Coaches
- *The Bowen Story* -
A Pictorial History Of The Bowen Coach Group

Andrew Roberts

BREWIN BOOKS

Published by Brewin Books Ltd
Studley, Warwickshire B80 7LG
in 2004

www.brewinbooks.com

© Andrew Roberts 2004

All rights reserved.

The moral right of the author has been asserted.

ISBN 1 85858 248 2

British Library Cataloguing in Publication Data
A Catalogue record for this book is available from the British Library.

Typeset in Times
Printed in Great Britain by
Alden Press Limited

Contents

The Bowen Story – Part 1, 1928-1976   1

The Bowen Story – Part 2, 1976 onwards   61

Fleet list for L F Bowen Companies   134

Arnolds Coaches, Tamworth   140

Fleet list for Arnold's Coaches   144

Acknowledgements

Thanks to the following for their much appreciated assistance with this publication.

Mr Bowen's daughter; Mrs B Bates and grand daughter; Mrs B Fortune
Alan Mills of the PSV circle for providing fleet list information

ATPH for providing some of the photographs used from the Association of Transport Photographers and Historians collection. (Visit the ATPH web-site: www.transportphotos.com for details of the collection.)

And to all who have loaned photographs and other material and have given permission for pictures from their collections to be reproduced.

The Bowen Story Part 1, 1928-1976 – Building an Empire

Leslie Frank Bowen was born in 1904, his father, William Bowen was a butcher by trade and the family lived in the Lozells district of Birmingham, which is where Leslie spent his early years, and attended school.

Mr L F Bowen

Les drove for a local company for a time after leaving school, and then in 1928, at the age of 24 he decided to start his own road haulage business. He purchased a second-hand Ford model T truck for the sum of £50.00, of which he borrowed £20.00 under a hire purchase arranged by Mr H Jackson Wray of Wray and Company (Birmingham) Limited. Mr Wray had faith in Leslie Bowen as a hard working young man who would honour his obligations and make a success of his new venture. This Leslie did throughout his life – always paying his way.

The early days of the haulage business were operated from a site on the Coventry Road in Yardley and concentrated on the carriage of meat to and from the Birmingham central market. Within ten years a fleet of six Dennis lorries were owned and it was decided that new, larger, premises were needed. A suitable place was found at 196 Anthony Road in Saltley that was owned by W. Stilgoe who operated coaches under the name of "Royal George Coaches". Pressure was exerted on Les Bowen to take the vehicles as well as the garage and almost overnight he became the owner of some coaches, which included an AEC, a Daimler and a Dennis together with some licences to run excursions and tours.

Before Mr Bowen had time to concentrate on his new business interest the second-world war intervened and the fleet was taken-over for forces transportation. The lorries too were involved in the war effort and Les Bowen became a meat allocater for the Ministry of food at Birmingham meat market.

Mr Bowen's taste for operating coaches had been whetted and a wartime contract to convey workers to the Austin factory was started. By the end of the war he had six coaches on the contract of which there were various makes including a couple of Maudslays, two Bedford WTB and a Leyland TS7 most being acquired via the War department.

Two lorries from Les Bowen's fleet: AOP 40 on the left is a Dennis and AOE 127 is a Commer, both date from around 1935.
Mrs B Fortune collection

After the war Les Bowen continued to operate his haulage fleet but with the post-war demand for travel he decided upon expansion of his coaching business. New vehicles were not easy to obtain, a permit being required, but Mr Bowen claimed that he had the first all-new post war fleet in Birmingham. The first new coach arrived in 1946, a Dennis Lancet fitted with 33-seat body by Santus of Wigan. The Santus bodywork must have impressed Mr Bowen as no less than 16 were purchased between 1947 and 1950. Most were mounted on Dennis Lancet III chassis but there were also three Maudslay Marathon 3s, a solitary Seddon and a Dennis Lance – which is believed to be the only Lance chassis that had a single-deck body as this chassis normally, had double-deck bodywork. The fleet name of "Superior Coaches" was added to the cream and maroon livery. This remained as a fleet name until the late 1970's, by which time it had evolved to "Superior Continental".

In 1947 the business of Payne's Ashted Coaches of Vauxhall were acquired for the sum of £1500.00. At around this time larger premises were needed for the expanding fleet and a move to 101 Cotterills Lane in Alum Rock was made. In 1950 a covered garage building was erected using two blister hangars that were bought from Biggin Hill airfield. The hangars remained in place until 1985 when they were damaged by a heavy fall of snow. The cost for the repair was going to be in the region of £90,000.00 so it was decided to demolish the building. This site, although extensively modified, is still currently the head office of the company.

AEC and Bedford chassis made-up the fleet throughout the 1950's, two AEC Regals fitted with the elegant Burlingham Seagull body were purchased, one in 1952 and the other the following year. Further Burlingham Seagulls were added in 1956 and 1957, this time on Bedford SB chassis. At the time, a policy of replacing part of the fleet after about two years service was established and more Bedford SBs were added in 1958 and 1959 this time with Duple Vega bodywork.

A further acquisition took place in 1958 when the business of Albert Winwood of Yardley was taken-over. Winwood's was a small operation based in Flora Road, that ran just two or three coaches. With the business came further licences to operate excursions and a summer express service to Margate. Two coaches were involved in the deal, an AEC Reliance – Burlingham and a Duple bodied Bedford SB, but these were only kept for a few months.

At around the same time further expansion of the haulage side of the business took place when a new contract was taken on with ICI, this involved around twenty vehicles, mainly Seddons that were painted in ICI's own livery. The contract was for the delivery of paint to various locations around the country and was operated for around ten years after which Mr Bowen decided to concentrate all of his energies on coach travel.

The size of the coach fleet was nearly doubled in 1962 when Arnolds Coaches Limited of Two Gates, Tamworth was taken-over. John Arnold (who was always known as "Jack") started his business in the early 1920's, originally as a taxi firm and he acquired his first coach in 1926. Les Bowen had been a long-time friend of the Arnolds and acquired the business after the death of Jack Arnold. Twelve coaches mostly Bedford chassis, the Two Gates depot and a travel agency in Tamworth town centre was included in the deal.

The heyday for coach travel was from the post-war years up to the 1970's. Unlike today, not all families owned a car and many relied upon coaches to transport them to their summer holiday resort and on day excursions throughout the year. Prior to de-regulation in the early 1980's, a road service licence was required to operate an express service, excursion or tour. The licences were issued by the area Traffic Commissioner and each licence determined the route, timetable and where passengers could be picked-up and set-down. The traffic commissioner also approved the fares and could impose a limit on the number of coaches operated to a particular

One of the two coaches acquired with the business of Winwood's: ROX 184, a 1955 AEC Reliance with 41-seat Burlingham Seagull body.
R H G Simpson

The only vehicle acquired with the Newton's of Perry Barr business: 917 GOF a 1962 Bedford SB with Duple Super Vega 41-seat body.
P M Photography

destination. Any changes had to be agreed in advance and applications for new licences, and changes to existing ones, had to be supported by evidence of demand from potential customers. All applications were heard at the traffic courts and often incurred objections from competing companies - the whole process could prove rather lengthy.

Some of the take-overs made by L F Bowen did not involve any vehicles; they were made to acquire the operator's licences thus enabling further expansion of the pick-up area and destinations offered. Permission still however had to be sought from the Traffic Commissioner to take-over another operators licences. One such take-over was that of Newton's Coach Services of Perry Barr in 1964. Newton's held licences for express services, which enabled Mr Bowen to develop his catchment area to include the North West of the City of Birmingham. Only one vehicle was taken into the L F Bowen fleet the remainder being sold. The licences for excursions were not required and also disposed of.

Bedford and AEC continued to be the favoured choice for new coaches throughout the 1960's. In 1961 a fleet of seven Harrington Crusader bodied Bedford SBs replaced the Duple bodied SB's from 1958 and 1959. Plaxton's Panorama design was fitted to two AEC Reliances and in 1965 five more AEC Reliances were purchased, this time with the Harrington Grenadier body. These were featured in company publicity and were promoted as "motorway" type coaches. Most new purchases at this time were made through the dealership of E J Baker (Dorking) Ltd; Mr Bowen preferred to deal with just one organisation.

Keeping the fleet in first-class condition at all times was very important and in 1968 a new workshop was erected at the rear of the Cotterills Lane premises which allowed up to five coaches to be maintained or repaired at any one time. The excellent condition of the fleet was also achieved through no vehicle being any older than four years in age and each driver being allocated his own coach, the presentation for which he would be responsible. The Arnold's of Tamworth vehicles were also maintained at Cotterills Lane. This fleet consisted of Bedford and Ford chassis as much of the work undertaken involved local contracts to which this type of vehicle was suited. It was common for coaches to be transferred to Tamworth from the L F Bowen fleet after two or three year's service.

1968 saw further expansion when the business of Eatonways, Small Heath was acquired. Again no vehicles were included but Eatonways held over 300 licences, which enabled a major expansion of Bowen's express routes and excursions programme. Eatonways was established in the early 1930's by Frederick Eaton and originally operated from Chapman Road in Small Heath but later moved to larger premises on the Coventry Road. The fleet livery was cream and brown and most vehicles were acquired new with Leyland and Bedford chassis the main choice, although a number of AECs were also purchased. The Foy Group acquired the company in 1965 and at some stage another depot was established in Berkeley Road East. At around this time a separate fleet under the Eatonways Travel name was established to operate a service from central Birmingham to Elmdon Airport. Eatonways also had a travel shop on the Coventry Road at Hay Mills, which was retained by Bowens. A separate business, L F Bowen (Small Heath) Limited was set-up with one or two coaches allocated to it from the main fleet.

At this time in the company's history the number of licences held meant L F Bowen was the major independent operator providing summer express services and excursions. All of the company's activities were based on recreational travel as no schools or works contracts were undertaken. In the summer months the company would send more than 60 coaches each Saturday to coastal resorts around the country and more than 15,000 passengers were carried on day excursions throughout each year. Extended tours were also operated and private hire also kept the ever expanding fleet busy.

In 1969 one of the largest acquisitions took place when the business of Stockland Garage Limited of Erdington, and its subsidiary Gliderways Coaches of Smethwick, was taken-over. The licences of Stockland were kept but none of its vehicles or the garage at Stockland Green. Six Leyland coaches from Gliderways were absorbed into the L F Bowen fleet and continued to operate from the original Gliderways depot in Vince Street, Bearwood.

Stockland had been established in the 1930's by Mr J H McLaughlin and was later joined by Mr I V McLaughlin. Control of Burley's Garage of Lozells was gained in 1946 and this operation continued as a separate business. Gliderways, Bearwood was purchased in the early 1960's and Sandwell Motors of Handsworth were taken-over in 1966. Stockland were well known for their European touring programme and the cream and blue livery of their coaches featured a display of European flags on the boot doors. These tours were continued under the L F Bowen title and Stockland's small booking office next to the garage on Marsh Hill was retained until new larger premises were opened on the corner of Marsh Hill and Slade Road – these remained as a Bowen Travel Agency until October 2003.

Gliderways had been operating since the early 1920's and was established by H Morris. The company was one of the most well known, and respected, in the area and operated day excursions, summer express routes and private hire. Although other types were operated, Gliderways were famous for their fleet of Harrington bodied Leylands and their grey and maroon livery was always immaculately presented. L F Bowen established a new company, L F Bowen (Gliderways) Limited in 1973; some vehicles from the main fleet were transferred to the company, painted in a grey and maroon livery, to replace the coaches acquired from the original Gliderways fleet. Subsequent vehicles for this operation were however painted white and red or cream and maroon.

February 1970 saw another AEC Reliance enter the fleet; this vehicle SOL 832H, was fitted with a 51-seat body built in Portugal by Salvador Caetano. The continental design looked very modern for the time and the specification of the Caetano body included many items as standard that were considered as optional extras on a British body. The

609 BOH, a 1960 Ford Thames with Burlingham 37-seat body, demonstrates the display of European flags incorporated into the Stockland livery. P Southern collection

interior had many areas trimmed in fabric rather than formica, full draw curtains added to the luxurious feel – as did the livery, which was applied in continental fashion with maroon stripes on the cream base. The Caetano range of bodies was imported into the UK by the Loughborough based Moseley Group dealership and the first example must have impressed Les Bowen because over the next few years more than 50 Caetano bodied coaches were purchased for the Bowen Group fleets.

Plaxton and Duple bodies also continued to be purchased in the 1970's on AEC, Leyland, Bedford and Ford chassis additionally, one very rare coach joined the fleet in August 1971; AOH 561K was one of only nine UTIC Tagus vehicles imported into the UK. The Utic, like Cateano, was constructed in Portugal and imported by The Moseley Group; it was an integral design that had a rear-mounted AEC engine. For reasons unknown AOH 561K only stayed with Bowens for two months but two more of the type were purchased in 1974 after serving with Supreme Coaches (Bonas and Son Ltd) of Coventry. These two were operated for about twelve months during which time they retained Supreme's smart two tone blue livery.

Two used examples of the rare UTIC-AEC coaches entered the fleet in 1974: GDU 66L is pictured when operating for it's original owner Supreme Coaches of Coventry.
P M Photography

In November 1973 Flight's Tours Limited, one of the oldest established coach business in Birmingham, was taken-over. The purchase included Flight's fleet of 14 AEC coaches, its licences and the garage in Berners Street, Lozells. Frank Flight established a taxi business around 1913 and later acquired a vehicle that could be used as a lorry during the week and a bus at weekends. Additional coaches were purchased and, before the Second World War a fleet of five had been built-up. The business originally operated from 114 Victoria Road in Aston but in 1961, the business of H Grimsley was acquired and the combined fleets then operated from Grimsley's garage in Berners Street, Lozells. Two other operators were also acquired by Flight's – Dalton's Coaches and Sugdens, both were based in Handsworth. L F Bowen acquired Flight's Tours Limited on 1st November in 1973 and a new company L F Bowen (Flights Coaches) Limited was formed and the coaches remained in Flight's cream and black livery with "L F Bowen" fleet name, although subsequent vehicles allocated to that depot were in cream and maroon livery. Berners Street was eventually closed in 1978 and the coaches transferred to Cotterills Lane, Alum Rock.

Throughout the 1970's L F Bowen provided the team coach for Aston Villa F.C., this contract was taken over from the Flight's business. Executive specification coaches were used, initially one of two Bedford YRTs with Caetano bodies which joined the fleet in 1972 and then a Leyland Leopard with Plaxton body which was new in 1975. For a number of years Bowens also sponsored the "Player of the Year" award.

In 1976 Les Bowen decided that it was time to retire. From the post-war years he had gradually expanded his coach business, starting with the few vehicles acquired from Stilgoe's to eventually become the largest independent operator in the area – operating over 70 coaches from four depots in Birmingham, Tamworth and Bearwood. His son-in law, Bernard Hopkins, who was also a director of the company responsible for operational and licensing matters, had assisted Mr Bowen throughout these years. Bernard Hopkins remained with the company, under its new ownership.

During his time in the coaching industry, Mr Bowen was a member of the Passenger Vehicle Operators Association and, in 1970, he was elected as the National President. Mr Bowen always enjoyed driving and was very proud of his cars. Throughout his retirement he and Mrs Bowen continued to travel extensively mainly throughout England and Scotland. Eventually, owing to Mrs Bowen's health they moved from their Birmingham home to a bungalow in Cheshire where they would be near to one of their daughters, Mrs Barbara Bates. Sadly Mrs Bowen died in 1980 and Les Bowen in May 1991.

1946 - GOJ 424 the first brand-new coach purchased after the Second World War. It had a Dennis Lancet chassis with a 33-seat body by Santus of Wigan. *Roy Marshall*

1948 – HOV 426 Dennis Lance chassis with 33-seat Santus body – pictured when new outside the Dennis sales agent. The Lance chassis was usually fitted with double-deck bus bodies and this is believed to be the only one that received a single-deck coach body. *Robin Hannay*

1948 – HOP 749 Dennis Lancet III chassis with Santus 33-seat body – pictured near Epsom in 1952. *NA3T / ATPH*

1949 – JOL 375 another 33-seat Santus this time built upon a Maudslay Marathon 3 chassis. Fifteen Santus bodied coaches were purchased between 1946 and 1950. *NA3T / ATPH*

1949 – JOH 946 Seddon P6 Mk IV chassis with Santus 31-seat body. Note the glazed roof panels and the full-length emergency exit door fitted to this vehicle. *NA3T / ATPH*

Maudslay, JOL 375 and Seddon, JOH 946 are pictured whilst parked-up somewhere in London. *NA3T / ATPH*

1950 – KOE 478 Dennis Lancet III chassis with 33-seat Santus body. This was one of the first coaches in the fleet with a "full-fronted" body. *Roy Marshall*

1950 – KOE 794 another Dennis Lancet III with Santus 33-seat body. The polished metal trim disguised an otherwise plain front panel. *Roy Marshall*

An early 1950's view of 101 Cotterills Lane, Alum Rock - the covered garage building was constructed in 1950 using two blister hangars that came from RAF Biggin Hill. *Mrs B Bates collection*

A closer view of the garage with Santus bodied Dennis coaches in view including KOE 478, GOV 658, HOV 426, KOC 668 and KOB 748. Doors were fitted at both ends of the garage to enable coaches to be driven through the building. *Mrs B Bates collection*

1953 – NOF 550 AEC Regal IV chassis with elegant Burlingham Seagull 37-seat body. This picture was taken at Earls Court in London where the coach was exhibited by AEC at the Commercial Motor Show. At the show it was displayed as a "Maudslay Regal" – AEC had by that time acquired the Maudslay Company and a small number of Regals were built as Maudslays – NOF 550 however was "re-badged" as an AEC before it entered service. *N Wood collection*

1956 – TOB 336 Bedford SBG chassis with 41-seat Burlingham Seagull body. One of three identical coaches purchased in 1956 – five more followed the next year. *Mrs B Bates collection*

1959 – XOJ 609 Bedford SB3 chassis with Duple Super Vega 41-seat body. Eight of these coaches were acquired during 1958 and 1959 and they replaced the Bedford – Burlinghams of 1956 and 1957. *P M Photography*

In 1961 a total of seven new Bedford SB's were purchased with Harrington Crusader 41-seat bodies. Five are pictured here awaiting collection from the supplying dealer, E J Baker of Dorking. *Mrs B Bates collection*

Mr L F Bowen (right) receives the keys for his new acquisitions. Mrs Bowen and representatives of Harrington's and Vauxhall Motors are also present. *Mrs B Bates collection*

Another picture of the five Bedford – Harrington's as they travel in convoy along the M1 en-route to Birmingham. What a different scene to today's motorway conditions with hardly any traffic and note also the absence of central carriageway crash barriers. *Mrs B Bates collection*

793 COE, one of the Bedford SB – Harrington Crusaders was entered in the National Coach Rally at Blackpool - it is pictured here whilst travelling along the Promenade, just past the famous Tower. *NA3T / ATPH*

Another view of 793 COE at the Rally, the driver is manoeuvring the coach through the driving tests that were part of the National Coach Driver of the Year contest. *NA3T / ATPH*

A rear view of 798 COE shows the attractive lines of the Harrington body. These coaches had the Bedford SB8 chassis, which used Leyland's 400 diesel engine – previous SB's operated by the company had Bedford petrol engines. *Mrs B Fortune collection*

Another of the 1961 Harrington Crusader – Bedfords, 794 COE, is seen leaving Wembley Stadium. *R H G Simpson*

1963 – 794 JOB AEC Reliance chassis with 51-seat Plaxton Panorama body.
PM Photography

When first launched in 1958, the Panorama was a striking design featuring large side windows – these would become a standard feature of British coach designs of the 1960's and 1970's.

1963 – 906 HOX Bedford SB8 chassis with Harrington Crusader 41-seat body. This coach had the Mk III version of the Crusader design; the main difference from the previous version being the longer side window bays and revised moulding scheme. *A Roberts collection*

Private Hire Handbook – 1965. This useful 36-page book listed itineraries and descriptions of destinations for private party organisers.

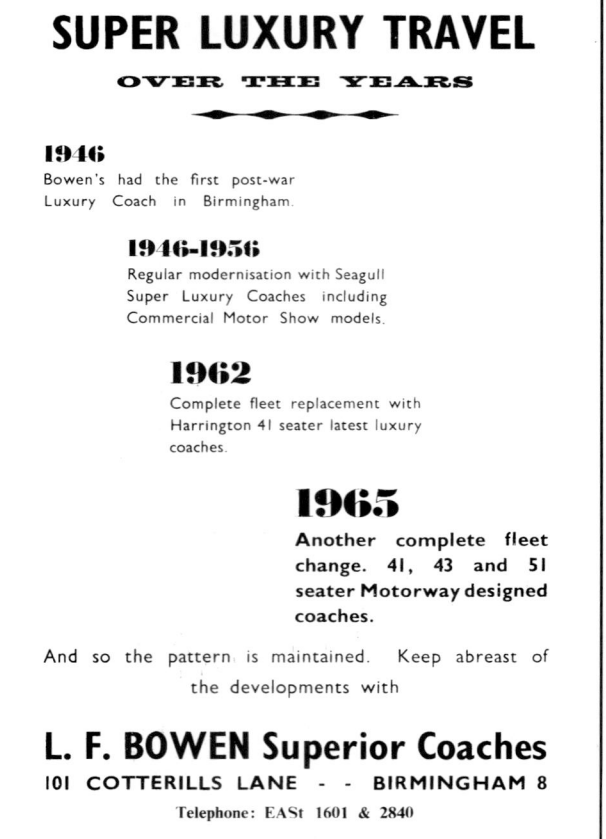

1965 – Collecting six new Harrington bodied AEC Reliances, BOF 854 – 859C. On the left is Bernard Hopkins (son-in law of L F Bowen), Mr L F Bowen and Mrs Bowen is receiving flowers from representatives of the manufacturer and dealer. *Mrs B Bates collection*

An official Harrington Coachbuilders photograph of BOF 854C. The Harrington Grenadier is regarded as one of the classic coach designs of the 1960's. *Mrs B Bates collection*

1965 – Two of the new Harrington Grenadier bodied AEC Reliances were entered in the British Coach Rally at Brighton. BOF 857C was entry number 27 and is pictured on Madeira Drive.
NA3T / ATPH

BOF 856C was the second coach to represent the company at Brighton as entry number 50.
NA3T / ATPH

The coach rally takes place over a weekend each April and includes a series of driving tests that lead to the "Coach Driver of the Year" finals on Sunday afternoon. The driver of BOF 856C reverses his vehicle during the tests on Madeira Drive. *Mrs B Fortune collection*

Another view of BOF 856C at the rally – note that tables are fitted. *NA3T / ATPH*

Three of the 1965 AEC – Harringtons were of the longer 36ft long versions with 51-seat bodies, as represented here by BOF 855C. *RHG Simpson*

BOF 859C was one of three shorter length 41-seat examples of the Harrington Grenadier – AEC Reliance combination. This coach is currently undergoing restoration (see page 133). *PM Photography*

A 1960's view of 101 Cotterills Lane, Alum Rock – canopies have been erected over the petrol sales area and the boards along the front advertise forthcoming trips. *Mrs B Bates collection*

1966 – GOH 494D AEC Reliance chassis with Plaxton Panorama I 51-seat body. Three Plaxton bodied coaches joined the fleet in 1966, two on AEC Reliance chassis and the other a 29-seater on Bedford VAS1 chassis. *M J Perry*

1967 – JOE 189E another AEC Reliance with 51-seat Plaxton Panorama I body, this was the only new coach purchased in 1967. *PM Photography*

1968 – ORF 484F, one of two Bedford VAM70 chassis with 45-seat Plaxton Panorama I bodies to be placed into the Tamworth based subsidiary fleet of Arnold's Coaches. *R H G Simpson*

Another representative of the Arnold's fleet, NUX 111G a Bedford VAM70 chassis with Duple Viceroy 45-seat body which was acquired from Whittle's of Highly in 1971. *RHG Simpson*

1969 – ROA 729G, one of four more AEC Reliances added to the fleet all with Plaxton's latest Panorama Elite design body seating 51. Unusually these coaches had leather cloth seat coverings rather than the usual moquette. *Photobus*

1969 – ROA 730G AEC Reliance chassis with 51-seat Plaxton Panorama Elite body – note that the fleet name is now "Superior Continental". *Photobus*

When Stockland Garage of Erdington was taken-over in 1969 no vehicles from its fleet were acquired but six coaches from the associated Gliderways business were absorbed into the L F Bowen fleet.

6912 HA was one of two 1963 Leyland PSU3/3R chassis with 49-seat Harrington Grenadier bodies. The chassis of both of these vehicles were originally built for export and were salvaged from a sunken ship bound for Australia.
B French collection

8757 HA was one of two 1964 Leyland PSU3/3RT chassis with Harrington Grenadier 51-seat bodies.
P Southern collection

The newest of the Gliderways vehicles acquired were two 1966 Leyland Leopard chassis with 49-seat Plaxton Panorama I bodies, as represented here by FHA 903D.
R H G Simpson

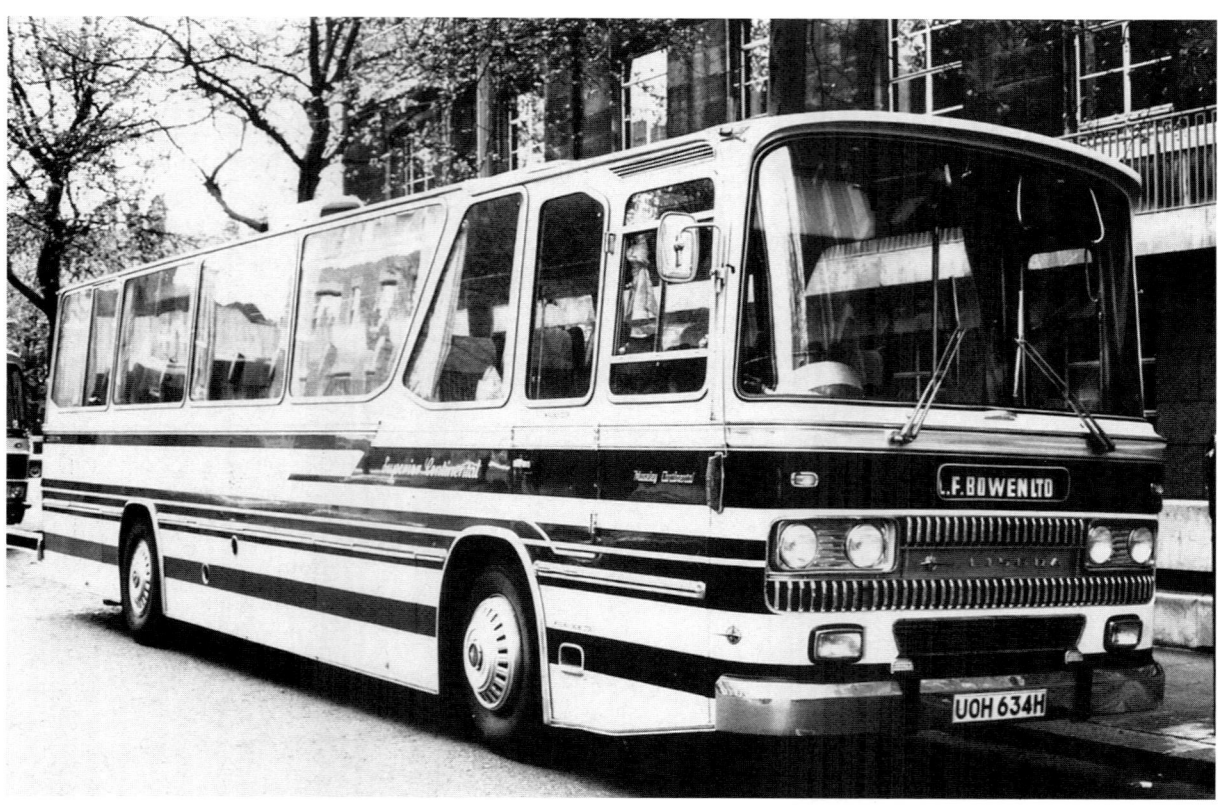

1970 – UOH 634H AEC Reliance chassis with Caetano Lisboa 51-seat body. Three vehicles of this type entered the fleet in 1970 and were the first of what would be a large number of coaches purchased with the Portuguese Salvador Caetano body. *Photobus*

The Caetano body offered modern styling for its time as well as many items as standard which were regarded as extras on British built bodies including, wheel trims, and the continental style striped livery. The interior of the body had areas covered in fabric, rather than formica and curtains were usually fitted as standard. *R H G Simpson*

1971 – Seven Bedford YRQ chassis with Duple Viceroy 45-seat bodies were taken into the fleet, including YOA 694J which is pictured waiting to depart for North Devon – a destination once featured in the express service programme. *R H G Simpson*

1971 – YOJ 227J Bedford YRQ chassis with 45-seat Duple Viceroy body. All seven of these coaches were transferred to the Arnold's subsidiary in 1974. *Photobus*

1971 – XBF 328J Ford R226 chassis with Caetano Estoril 53-seat body, one of two for the Arnold's fleet. *R H G Simpson*

1971 – ERF 207K, another Arnold's vehicle, Bedford YRQ chassis with Duple Viceroy 45-seat body. *Photobus.*

A Pictorial History of the Bowen Coach Group

1971 – WVP 704J AEC Reliance chassis with 51-seat Caetano Lisboa body. Ten Caetano bodied coaches joined the L F Bowen fleet in 1971, two on AEC Reliance chassis and eight on Ford R226, all featured the re-styled Caetano body for the 1971 season. *M J Perry*

A total of sixteen new coaches were acquired in 1972, a mixture of AEC Reliance and Bedford chassis all with Caetano bodywork. This picture shows twelve coaches waiting to be collected from Moseley's of Loughborough who were, at the time, the UK distributor of Cateano bodied coaches. *Mrs B Bates Collection*

1972 – BOA 945K AEC Reliance chassis with 51-seat Caetano Lisboa body.
M J Perry

An offside view of BOA 945K, the striped livery application was a feature of the Caetano body. As can be seen on this and the facing page various styles were applied: the version on BOA 945K (and sister vehicles BOA 943, 4 and 6K) was however rather more restrained than some of the others. *Photobus*

The 1972 intake of coaches included nine Bedford YRQ chassis with 45-seat Caetano bodies, including CON 280K. Salvador Caetano named its models after Portuguese towns and cities, this shorter version was known as the Cascais. *A Roberts collection*

1972 – COA 748K AEC Reliance chassis with 57-seat Caetano Lisboa body. This and sister coach, COA 749K, were the first 40ft (12-metre) long coaches purchased by the company. *Photobus*

L.F. Bowen Ltd

1972 BRITISH & CONTINENTAL TOURS

DIRECT from the MIDLANDS

1972 brochure for British and Continental holidays.

A 1972 view of 101 Cotterills Lane, Alum Rock, further modifications to the building and forecourt are evident when compared to the view on page 23. The garage part of the building was demolished in 1985 after a heavy fall of snow damaged the hangars that formed the roof. Additional offices were eventually built along the front and to the rear of the building and although coaches are no longer based there the site currently remains the head office of the company. *Mrs B Bates collection*

Representing the Arnold's of Tamworth fleet, COG 32K was one of nine Bedford YRQs with 45-seat Caetano Cascais bodies that were new to the L F Bowen fleet in 1972. *Photobus*

COG 34K, another coach from the same batch – all nine were transferred to the Arnold's subsidiary in 1974. Note the different position of the headlights when compared to COG 32K. *Photobus*

1972 – FOK 824L Bedford YRT chassis with Caetano Estoril II body. This coach was built to executive specification and was the first in the fleet to have the series II version of the Caetano Estoril body.

This and similar coach, HOM 471L which was delivered in 1973, were used for continental tours, private hire and later to transport the Aston Villa Football Team when that contract was continued after the acquisition of Flight's Tours.

The specification included reclining seats – eight of which were situated around tables, television, audio system, rear lounge with conference table, fridge, hot and cold water and a cocktail cupboard.

Mr Bowen claimed that they were the first true "Executive" coaches to operate in Birmingham. FOK 824L was featured on BBC Midlands TV "Home James" programme when new.

Superior Coaches – The Bowen Story

1973 – HOM 471L, the second of the executive specification Caetano bodied Bedford YRTs, was delivered in time to represent the company at the British Coach Rally in Brighton. *Mrs B Bates collection*

Mr L F Bowen is pictured with HOM 471L at the rally receiving the Moseley Continental trophy from the Mayor of Brighton. *Mrs B Bates collection*

A Pictorial History of the Bowen Coach Group

1973 – A new company, L F Bowen (Gliderways) Limited, was formed to operate from the former Gliderways depot in Bearwood. Caetano Lisboa bodied AEC Reliance, UOH 635H was one of thirteen coaches transferred from the L F Bowen fleet and painted in Gliderways grey and maroon livery.
Credits: Photobus, J Wensley, B French Collection

L F Bowen (Gliderways) Limited XOH 72J, a 1971 Ford R226 with Caetano Estoril 53-seat body. *Photobus*

Another of the vehicles transferred to the new Gliderways subsidiary, AOM 15K is a Ford R226 with 53-seat Caetano Estoril body new in 1971. *R H G Simpson*

1973 – GOK 958L Bedford YRT chassis with 53-seat Caetano Estoril II body, one of four new coaches in 1973 for L F Bowen (Gliderways) Limited. *J Mudge*

1973 – L F Bowen (Gliderways) Limited HOM 472L another Bedford YRT with Caetano Estoril II 53-seat body. *PM Photography*

The business of Flight's Tours was taken-over on 1st November 1973 and a new company formed L F Bowen (Flights Coaches) Limited. Fourteen coaches were included, one of the oldest was FOP 702D a 1966 AEC Reliance with Plaxton Panorama I body. It is pictured here when operating for its former owner. *R H G Simpson*

Another of the ex-Flight's coaches, YOB 740J was an AEC Reliance with Plaxton Panorama Elite II body. Although usually operated as a 51-seater, in this picture tables are fitted. All of the former Flights coaches retained their cream and black livery but with L F Bowen fleet names. *R H G Simpson*

L F Bowen (Flights Coaches) Limited YOB 720J, a 57-seat Plaxton Panorama Elite II bodied AEC Reliance. This coach is pictured whilst loading passengers in Great Yarmouth when operating on a summer express service. *P M Photography*

CVP 750K, another L F Bowen (Flights Coaches) AEC Reliance with Plaxton Panorama Elite II body. This and CVP 770K were the two newest of the coaches acquired. A feature of the Flights fleet was the inclusion of the figure 7 in the registration number. *M J Perry*

Flight's operated the Team Coach for Aston Villa Football Club and L F Bowen continued this contract. Coaches were also provided to transport fans to away matches and in this picture; former Flight's UOM 707H is at the back of a long line of coaches waiting to depart from Villa Park. *Mrs B Bates collection*

Flight's vehicles were always smartly presented and they were regularly entered in the British Coach Rally. This picture shows CVP 770K, prior to the Bowen take-over at Aston Hall with its collection of trophies awarded at the 1972 rally including "highest placed standard coach", "winner of class E in the Concours D'Elegance", the Plaxton trophy and the Kirkby trophy. Drivers, George Doige (in the kilt) and Malcolm Griffith are seen with the coach. *P Southern collection*

1973 – HOM 467L Bedford YRT chassis with 53-seat Caetano Estoril II body, one of ten delivered to the L F Bowen fleet in 1973. *Photobus*

The Arnold's fleet received four similar coaches in 1973, as represented by GOE 835L. *Photobus*

1974 brochure for British and Continental holidays

A Pictorial History of the Bowen Coach Group

L. F. Bowen (Gliderways) Ltd
316 BEARWOOD ROAD, SMETHWICK, WARLEY,
WEST MIDLANDS
(RING 021-429 2388)

**SKEGNESS SERVICE
(AND BUTLIN'S CAMP)**

Departures: Saturdays during July and August

Bearwood, Dawson Street	07.30
Warley, The Beech Tree	07.35
Causeway Green, Hen & Chickens	07.40
West Smethwick, Mallin Street	07.45
Erdington, Stockland Garage	08.00
Kingstanding, Kingstanding Hotel	08.06
Washwood Heath, Fox & Goose	08.20
SKEGNESS, Butlin's Camp Arrive	13.55
Depart	14.30
SKEGNESS, Lumley Road Arrive	13.47
Depart	14.38

* RETURN FARES
Adults £4.75   Children £2.40

WESTON-SUPER-MARE SERVICE

Departures: Saturdays during Last Saturday in May, June, July, August and September

Chelmsley Wood, Junction Chester Rd./Coleshill Heath Rd.	07.30
Chelmsley Wood, Junction Chester Road/Cooks Lane	07.35
Washwood Heath, Fox & Goose	07.45
Castle Vale, Tangmere Drive/Chester Road	07.50
Erdington, Stockland Garage	08.00
Kingstanding, Kingstanding Hotel	08.05
Bearwood, Dawson Street	08.30
West Smethwick, Mallin Street	08.35
Causeway Green, Hen & Chickens	08.40
Warley, The Beech Tree	08.45
Harborne, Duke of York	08.50
WESTON, Locking Road Car Park Arrive	
Depart	

* RETURN FARES
Adults £4.15   Children £2.10

Incorporating:
L. F. BOWEN LTD. (Head Office)
101 Cotterills Lane,
Alum Rock,
Birmingham, B8 3SA
Telephone 021-327 5921

L. F. BOWEN LTD.
2 Marsh Hill,
Erdington,
Birmingham, B23 7DR
Telephone 021-373 7415

L. F. BOWEN TRAVEL CENTRE
900 Coventry Road,
Hay Mills,
Birmingham, B10 0UA
Telephone 021-772 3241

L. F. BOWEN (Flights Coaches)
205 Berners Street, Lozells,
Birmingham, B19 2DU
Telephone 021-554 6375

* Fares subject to Traffic Commissioner's Approval
Passengers are recommended to take out Insurance to cover Cancellation Charges, Luggage, Illness, Etc.
Full Details on Application

L F Bowen (Gliderways) Limited leaflet for summer express services to Skegness and Weston-Super-Mare – circa 1974.

L. F. Bowen (Flights Coaches) Ltd
205 BERNERS STREET, BIRMINGHAM B19 2DU
(RING 021-554 6375)

GREAT YARMOUTH, CORTON-ON-SEA, GORLESTON, GUNTON HALL, HOPTON-ON-SEA, LOWESTOFT

Departures: Every Saturday from Last Saturday in May to Last Saturday in September

Lozells, Coach Station, Berners Street	06.45
Handsworth, Soho Road/Murdoch Road	07.00
West Bromwich, Dartmouth Square	07.14
West Bromwich, Hills Garage, Carters Green	07.17
West Bromwich, Old Church	07.23
Great Barr, Malt Shovel, Newton Road	07.28
Great Barr, Scott Arms	07.31
Kingstanding, Circle	07.37
Sutton, 64 Bus Terminus	07.42
Sutton Coldfield, W. H. Smith, Parade	07.47
Washwood Heath, Fox & Goose	08.00
Castle Bromwich, Timberley, Chester Road	08.05
Castle Bromwich, Bacons End Island	08.10
*Wednesbury, Market Place	07.15
*Walsall, Station Street	07.24
*Kings Norton, The Green	07.15
*West Heath, Man on the Moon	07.20
*Longbridge, Essoldo Cinema	07.26
*Northfield, Bell Hotel	07.31
*Selly Oak, Bentella's Corner	07.37
Hay Mills, 900 Coventry Road	07.45
Sheldon, Waggon & Horses	07.50
GREAT YARMOUTH, Beach Coach Station Arrive	13.30
Depart	14.00
GORLESTON, Baptist Church Arrive	13.24
Depart	14.06
HOPTON-ON-SEA, White Hart Inn Arrive	13.18
Depart	14.12
CORTON-ON-SEA, Hut Hotel Arrive	13.12
Depart	14.18
GUNTON HALL, Camp Gates Arrive	13.09
Depart	14.21
LOWESTOFT, Battery Green Coach Park Arrive	13.03
Depart	14.27

* RETURN FARES
From Points * to all destinations: Adults £7.25   Children £3.65
From other Taking-up-Points: Adults £7.00   Children £3.50

Incorporating:
L. F. BOWEN LTD. (Head Office)
101 Cotterills Lane,
Alum Rock,
Birmingham, B8 3SA
Telephone 021-327 5921

L. F. BOWEN LTD.
2 Marsh Hill,
Erdington,
Birmingham, B23 7DR
Telephone 021-373 7415

L. F. BOWEN (Gliderways) LTD.
316 Bearwood Road,
Smethwick,
Warley, West Midlands
Telephone 021-429 2388

L. F. BOWEN TRAVEL CENTRE
900 Coventry Road,
Hay Mills,
Birmingham, B10 0UA
Telephone 021-772 3241

* Fares subject to Traffic Commissioner's Approval
Passengers are recommended to take out Insurance to cover Cancellation Charges, Luggage, Illness, Etc.   Full Details on Application

L F Bowen (Flights Coaches) Limited leaflet for summer express service to Great Yarmouth – circa 1974.

1975 – JUK 949N Leyland Leopard chassis with Plaxton Panorama Elite III 53-seat body, one of four similar coaches for 1975. *Daniel Hill photography*

Two of the Plaxton bodied Leyland Leopards, JUK 948N and JUK 950N, were painted in Flights cream and black livery with L F Bowen "Executive Travel" fleet names. JUK 948N is pictured whilst on tour. *P M Photography*

1975 – JUK 950N was the second of the cream and black Leyland Leopard – Plaxtons.
P M Photography

Another view of JUK 950N, pictured whilst operating one of the many day excursions offered by the company. *P M Photography*

1975 JOH 951N Bedford YRT chassis with Caetano Estoril II 53 seat body, one of four delivered to the L F Bowen (Gliderways) Limited fleet in 1975. *J Wensley*

JOH 948N is another of the batch; these four coaches were painted white and red rather than the usual Gliderways livery of grey and maroon. *Photobus*

1975 – DRF 118N Bedford YRT chassis with 53-seat Plaxton Elite Express III body, one of four identical coaches for the Arnold's of Tamworth fleet. *Photobus*

Many of the colliery and factory services operated by Arnold's were registered as stage carriage routes. This status allowed the purchase of vehicles with the help of the bus grant scheme and this view of DRF 119N shows the "express" doors fitted to these four coaches. The twin folding doors were necessary for the wider entrance required as part of the bus grant scheme regulations. *Photobus*

1975 – LUK 85P Ford R1114 chassis with 53-seat Duple Dominant body. A total of nineteen vehicles of this type were taken into the Bowen Group fleets during 1975. *Photobus*

An off-side view of another of the batch, LUK 84P - the application of the livery was not quite as attractive on these vehicles, also the lack of polished wheel trims did not help their appearance. *P M Photography*

1975 – LOA 174P another Ford R1114 with Duple Dominant body. Although in maroon and cream livery with L F Bowen fleet names, this coach was one of five identical coaches allocated to the L F Bowen (Flights Coaches) fleet. *Photobus*

The Arnold's subsidiary received eight of the 1975 delivery of Ford R1114s with Duple bodies, as represented here by KVP 943P. *Photobus*

1975 – KOG 947P Leyland Leopard chassis with Plaxton Panorama Elite III body. This was the fourth of the Leyland Leopards taken into the fleet this year and was built to "Executive" specification with reclining seats, tables, toilet, Television, bar etc. *PM Photography*

KOG 947P was used on the Aston Villa Football team coach contract and is pictured here when new with Bill Fellows (Traffic Manager, Tamworth), Mr L F Bowen, Bernard Hopkins (Director) and Don Hipkiss (Traffic Manager, L F Bowen (Flights Coaches) Ltd). *Mrs B Bates collection*

1975 – LUK 10P AEC Reliance chassis with 53-seat Plaxton Panorama Elite III body. This and LUK 9P were the last new AEC coaches purchased. *PM Photography*

1975 – LUK 9 P AEC Reliance chassis with Plaxton Supreme 53-seat body. This coach had one of the first of Plaxton's Supreme series bodies, whilst sister vehicle LUK 10P had one of the last of the previous Elite III model. This picture shows the coach after it had been re-painted into the later version of the livery. *R H G Simpson*

1976 – MOC 19P Ford R1114 chassis with Caetano Estoril II 53-seat body, one of five delivered to L F Bowen (Gliderways) Ltd. All were painted in maroon and cream livery and some had L F Bowen fleet names – as shown on MOC 19P. *Photobus*

MOC 19P and MOC 20P were chosen to represent the company at the 1976 British Coach Rally. This batch of vehicles was the last new coaches to be delivered in the traditional maroon and cream livery. *P M Photography*

MOC 20P, with Gliderways fleet name, is pictured during the "road run" section of the rally.
B French Collection

Entries 31 and 32 - both coaches are pictured whilst on display at Madeira Drive in the "Concours d'Elegance". *P M Photograph*

Superior Coaches – The Bowen Story

L F Bowen Group day excursion brochures for 1976

L.F. Bowen Group
incorporating

L. F. BOWEN LIMITED
101 COTTERILLS LANE, ALUM ROCK, BIRMINGHAM B8 3SA
Telephone 021-327 5921

L. F. BOWEN LIMITED
2 MARSH HILL, ERDINGTON, BIRMINGHAM B23 7EP
Telephone 021-373 7415

L. F. BOWEN (FLIGHTS COACHES)
205 BERNERS STREET, LOZELLS, BIRMINGHAM B19 2DU
Telephone 021-554 6375

L. F. BOWEN TRAVEL CENTRE
900 COVENTRY ROAD, HAY MILLS, BIRMINGHAM B10 0UA
Telephone 021-772 3241

MARCH APRIL MAY JUNE 1976

Date	Destination	Time	Adult	Child
Saturday, March 13th	*Ideal Home Exhibition	07.45 hrs	£1·95	£1·30
Sunday, March 14th Half day tour	Warwick & Stratf... (Return for 18...			
Saturday, March 20th	*Ideal Home Exhi...			
Sunday, March 21st Half day tour	Evesham (Retur...			
Saturday, March 27th	*Ideal Home Exh...			
Sunday, March 28th Half day tour	Weston-super-M... Bourton-on-the-W...			
Saturday, April 3rd	*Ideal Home Exh... Liverpool (for ... incl. admissio...			
Sunday, April 4th Half day tour	Blackpool Worcester, Malv...			
Sunday, April 11th Half day tour	Rhyl Matlock & Dove...			
GOOD FRIDAY April 16th	Weston-super-M...			
EASTER SUNDAY April 18th Mid-morning tour Half day tour Evening tour	Weston-super-M... Windsor & Lond... Portsmouth Southsea Llangollen Circu... Symonds Yat Stratford			

L.F. Bowen Group
incorporating

L. F. BOWEN LIMITED
101 COTTERILLS LANE, ALUM ROCK, BIRMINGHAM B8 3SA
Telephone 021-327 5921

L. F. BOWEN LIMITED
2 MARSH HILL, ERDINGTON, BIRMINGHAM B23 7EP
Telephone 021-373 7415

L. F. BOWEN (FLIGHTS COACHES)
205 BERNERS STREET, LOZELLS, BIRMINGHAM B19 2DU
Telephone 021-554 6375

L. F. BOWEN TRAVEL CENTRE
900 COVENTRY ROAD, HAY MILLS, BIRMINGHAM B10 0UA
Telephone 021-772 3241

JULY AUGUST SEPT. OCTOBER 1976

Date	Destination	Time	Adult	Child
Sunday, July 4th	Weymouth	06.45 hrs	£2·00	£1·35
	Blackpool	07.45 hrs	£1·85	£1·25
	Weston-super-Mare	07.45 hrs	£1·70	£1·15
Mid morning tour	Llangollen via Horse Shoe Pass	08.45 hrs	£1·45	£1·00
Half day tour	*Trentham Gardens	13.00 hrs	£1·05	£0·70
Evening tour	Holt Fleet	17.00 hrs	£0·70	£0·50
Monday, July 5th	Lake Windermere	06.45 hrs	£2·05	£1·40
	Skegness	07.45 hrs	£1·90	£1·30
	*Windsor Safari Park	07.45 hrs	£1·70	£1·15
Half day tour	Worcester Circular	13.00 hrs	£0·70	£0·50
Tuesday, July 6th	Scarborough	06.45 hrs	£2·15	£1·45
	Llandudno	07.45 hrs	£1·75	£1·20
Half day tour	Tenbury, Bromyard & Stourport	13.00 hrs	£1·05	£0·70
Wednesday, July 7th	Weston-super-Mare	07.45 hrs	£1·70	£1·15
	Porthcawl	07.45 hrs	£1·85	£1·25
Half day tour	Cheltenham Circular	13.00 hrs	£1·20	£0·80
Thursday, July 8th	Weymouth	06.45 hrs	£2·00	£1·35
	Rhyl	07.45 hrs	£1·70	£1·15
	Southport	07.45 hrs	£1·70	£1·15
Half day tour	Ludlow & Hereford	13.00 hrs	£1·25	£0·85

Separate editions were also published for both L F Bowen (Gliderways) departures from the Bearwood area and Arnold's Coaches from Tamworth.

A view of the former Flight's Tours depot on Berners Street, Lozells with ex-Flight's AEC Reliance CVP 770K visible in the garage entrance. *C Ludford*

Leyland Leopard – Plaxton, JUK 948N and Ford R1114 – Duple LOA 175P are pictured in the open parking area adjacent to the Berners Street garage. *C Ludford*

Bowens on tour…Bedford YRT – Caetano Executive, FOK 824L is seen in the French town of Honfleur.

Bowens on tour…GOK 958L from the Gliderways fleet is pictured outside the Hotel Krone in Switzerland.
J Wensley

Bowens on tour…In its original livery, AEC Reliance – Plaxton Supreme LUK 9P is pictured in Paris at the Palais De Chaillot.
J Wensley

The Bowen Story Part 2, 1976 onwards – New owners and new horizons

Upon Les Bowen's retirement the company was sold to Moseley PSV Limited of Loughborough who were, at the time, one of the largest coach sales dealerships in the country. The Bowen fleet would be familiar to Moseley's, as they had supplied many of the coaches in recent years including all of the Salvador Caetano bodied coaches purchased throughout the 1970's. A new board of directors was appointed in addition to Bernard Hopkins who remained a Director of the company until his death in 1983. Other long serving members of the Bowen's management team of that era included General Manager, Arthur Butler, Peter Meadows who was manger of Arnold's, and later a director, and Phil Turner who had started as a driver and later ran the Express Service department – he still worked part time for many years after his retirement.

1976 saw further expansion for the group when Mann's Superlux Coaches of Smethwick was acquired. The deal included Mann's fleet of seven Duple bodied Bedford coaches and their depot located on Tram Way. William Mann had started his business career in the 1920's by hiring out bicycles to local children. The first coach, a Dennis, was acquired in 1930 and by the time of the Second World War six vehicles were operated under the name of Mermaid Coaches. The business grew after the war and the title of "Mann's Superlux Coaches" was adopted. The fleet originally operated from a garage in Westfield Road, Smethwick and premises were also owned in Holly Street. In 1967 a new garage and service station was opened on Rolfe Street and a booking office was also situated at 626 High Street. Mr Mann was joined in the business by his two sons, William and John, and his daughter, Mrs Peggy Wentworth – whose husband, John was also a director. The depot moved again the 1970's to a new unit on Tram Way. The Bowen Group acquired the company in October 1976, the coaches were transferred to Tamworth where they stayed only a short time; the depot however was relatively new and it was decided to transfer Bowen's coaches based at the original Gliderways Bearwood premises to there.

Four new coaches were added to the fleet in 1977, these were all Ford R-series with Caetano bodies and were the first to appear in a revised version of the livery. This retained the cream base but used a slightly brighter shade of red and also featured a yellow/gold stripe. The fleet name was simply "Bowens" in a new style of lettering which was common to all publicity material and company premises.

From 1978 the Bowens name was applied to all vehicles, the Arnold's and Gliderways identities being dropped. The former Flight's depot was closed in that year and all coaches from there were transferred to Cotterills Lane. A large intake of new coaches saw fifteen Bedford YMTs with Van-Hool Mc.Ardle bodies enter the fleet for the 1978 season. These were in a simplified version of the latest colours with the red and yellow applied in chevron style, upswept to the rear of the body. This style would be adopted as standard in the coming years.

The late 1970's and early 1980's saw a change in people's travel and holiday habits. The number of private cars and cheaper air-travel saw a reduced requirement for Express Services and Day Excursions. The company, at this time, underwent some streamlining in order to face up to the changing market place in which it traded. The coach fleet was reduced in size to match market requirements and the former Mann's depot was closed in 1980 leaving Cotterills Lane and Tamworth as the operational centres.

The new board of directors realised the potential of the company in the coach holiday market and this part of the business saw most expansion in the late 1970's and throughout the 1980's. 1979 saw a larger, 18-page, brochure produced entitled "Bowens in Britain" which featured many new destinations including Jersey, The Isle of Man and self-catering holidays on the Isle of Wight. A separate "Bowens on the Continent" brochure was also released.

1979 "Bowens in Britain" brochure.

To cope with the enlarged tours programme new offices were opened at Silhill House on the Coventry Road in Sheldon. These premises housed the holiday reservations and administration departments as well as the company accounts offices. When new office space became available at Cotterills Lane in 1988 both departments were transferred there and Silhill House was vacated.

During 1979 a London base was established. This operated from the Moseley Group's East Grinstead sales outlet and around 6 – 8 coaches were allocated there. The operation however only lasted for around two years. This year also saw more Bedford based coaches enter the fleet including five with Spanish-built Unicar bodies which was the latest Moseley Group offering.

From 1980 until 1992 the annual "Bowens Darts Championship" was held in Belgium. These innovative weekends attracted teams from all over the U.K. as well as some local ones from Belgium. At the height of the series as many as 1,000 people attended the three-day events.

In 1982 all coaches based at Cotterills Lane were transferred to the Fazeley Road, Tamworth depot where additional land was leased. This decision was taken as, at the time, most of the company's day coaching work originated from Tamworth, this included several colliery and works contracts as well as many coaches each day committed to schools contracts in the Aldridge area. One draw back to this decision was that many of the company's long serving Birmingham drivers were lost as they did not wish to travel to and from Tamworth each day.

The holiday programme continued to be expanded and the brochure produced for 1984 had now increased to 32-pages under the title of "Bowens the holiday makers". Most parts of the U.K. were offered as well as a larger choice of continental destinations and all holidays were now available from a greater pick-up area. A new holiday for that year was a 14-day tour to Yugoslavia centred in Opatija. Another new feature for 1984 was the introduction of a no smoking area on all tour coaches. A separate brochure "Bowens Breakaways" was launched for the first time, which included late season breaks for 1984 and spring 1985 mostly of 3 and 5 days duration. The main season brochure for 1985 was further enlarged and the programme was now covered by ABTA bonding. The pick-up area was extended beyond the West Midlands to include Derbyshire, Shropshire, Worcestershire and Greater Manchester.

A small Yorkshire company, Anderton's Coaches of Keighley was purchased in 1985 and four Bedford – Plaxton Coaches from the Bowens fleet were sent to supplement the existing fleet. The operation was however short lived – only lasting for about twelve months although pick-up points in Yorkshire for the tours programme were retained.

In 1987 a major contract was awarded the company to operate the car park to exhibition halls shuttle service at the National Exhibition Centre. This lucrative contract was operated for eight years and during the busiest shows, notably the Spring Fair and Motor Show, up to 30 coaches each day may be required.

Being part of the Moseley Group meant that the vehicle purchasing policy was dictated by what products the parent company was offering at the time. 1983 saw the arrival of two Dutch-built Bova Europa coaches with DAF running gear. These two vehicles would set the policy for all new purchases for the rest of the decade. Bova replaced the Europa model with the Futura and from 1984 more than 20 examples of this model would be placed into the Bowen fleet. A number of late model used vehicles, mainly Plaxton bodied Volvo B10Ms were also acquired which enabled the fleet to be modernised and bought up to the new standard specification of 49-seats with on-board toilet, drinks machines and videos. The first fully air-conditioned coaches arrived in 1992 and since then this has become standard equipment for all new purchases.

Another major contract for the company started in 1990 when the Express Service department became responsible for providing Haven Holidays clients with a coach transport option. Services to Haven Holiday Centres were offered on a nationwide basis, all reservations being made through Bowen's head office in Birmingham and coaches were contracted from other operators around the country. The contract ran for about six seasons. Haven, Butlins, Pontins and other holiday centres had featured in a Bowens "Coastline Holidays" series of brochures produced throughout the 1980's. These holidays made use of the company's Express Services and also featured hotel-based packages.

The 1990's saw the group diversify into other areas of travel. A few ABTA Travel Agencies were already operated but, in 1991, seven additional shops were taken-over from Don Everall Travel when they ceased trading. These acquisitions spread the Bowen Travel name across the West Midlands and paved the way for additional shops that were added over the coming years.

Further diversification took place in 1991 by the formation of a group travel department, its purpose being to provide tailor-made UK and Continental packages of accommodation and transport to group organisers. Wholesale packages to other coach operators were also made available and the incoming tourist market was also catered for – mainly dealing with visitors from North America.

One of the first brochures to be produced by the Group Travel Division.

In the mid 1990's the Moseley Group of companies restructured its business interests. Moseley (PCV) Limited, based in Pontefract continued to sell new Bova and Volvo – Van-Hool coaches as well as used vehicles from three outlets around the country. The Bowen group fell within Alf Moseley's Moseley PSV plc that also has extensive property interests.

At around this time Bowens purchasing policy for new coaches switched from Bova to the Scania K-series chassis with the Spanish built Irizar Century body, from 1994 to 1997 fifteen of the type were taken into the fleet.

In 1997 the Northampton based Yorks Travel Group was acquired. This company was highly respected locally and has a history going back to around 1924 when the York brothers established "The Easy Coach Company". The Yorks operation was similar to that of Bowens, originating from a coaching background and later diversifying into all areas of travel. The Yorks coach fleet totalled around 30 vehicles operated from a purpose-built depot in the village of Cogenhoe. Also included in the deal were fifteen travel agencies located across Northamptonshire and Buckinghamshire and a group and business travel department. Yorks own tours programme was integrated into the Bowens brochure although Yorks provide some coaches for tours throughout the season. In addition Yorks also offer late availability tours just from the Northamptonshire catchment area.

The parent company, Moseley PSV plc, re-entered the coach sales market in 1998 under the Alf Moseley Continental name with the Spanish-built Noge series of bodies built on M.A.N. chassis. The Bowens and Yorks fleet each received three of the type in that year which were the last new coaches to be delivered in the traditional cream and red livery. A new livery for the combined fleets was introduced in 1999; this featured a silver base with vinyl graphics in the shape of a ribbon along the side of the coach. New style lettering was introduced and the new image was adopted in all aspects of the Bowens and Yorks businesses.

AMC Sales also offered the Marcopolo body, the franchise having been acquired from the failed DSB Sales outlet. The Marcopolo was initially available only on Dennis Javelin chassis but later on M.A.N. – examples of which also featured in the Bowen group fleet. Alf Moseley disposed of the franchise for both bodies in 2003 and withdrew from the coach sales marketplace, leaving the way clear for the Bowen group to decide its own preferred future fleet replacements.

November 2000 saw further expansion when the Lincolnshire based Appleby's "Super Coach Holidays" programme was acquired. Appleby's were a large company involved with local bus services as well as coach touring and travel agents. The deal with Bowens involved the British and Continental holiday programme, fourteen Scania – Irizar coaches and eight travel agencies. The Appleby's holiday programme continues to operate independently and features around 500 departures from the Lincolnshire and Humberside area.

In June 2003 the Fazeley Road, Tamworth depot was vacated and the fleet moved to new premises based on the Lichfield Road Industrial Estate in Tamworth. These premises were formerly occupied by the Territorial Army and, as well as being more modern, offer significant improvements to the previous site with spacious offices, a modern covered workshop and plenty of hard standing for parking.

So what would Les Bowen think of the present day Bowen group? He should be proud that the Bowen name continues to expand and is recognised for providing value for money coaching holidays and travel not just throughout the West Midlands but also in Northamptonshire and Lincolnshire through its subsidiary companies.

The Birmingham based, Bowens Coaching Division, continues to offer all of the traditional services that would be familiar to Mr Bowen with private hire, day excursions and summer express routes still operated. The nation's second city, with the National Exhibition Centre, International Convention Centre and Indoor Arena also provides the company with high profile corporate work. Bowens have provided coaches to transport delegates and visitors to some of the major events that have taken place in recent years including the Eurovision Song Contest, World Figure Skating Contests and ITMA 2003. In 1998 when the G8 Summit took place in Birmingham, Bowens coaches transported dignitaries from around the globe – most notably President Bill Clinton. A number of contracts are also held for U.K. touring from incoming tour operators including Miki Travel and Japan Travel Bureau.

"Business Links" brochure for Corporate Travel clients.

Although the heritage of the company lies in its Birmingham roots it has evolved to become active in all aspects of the travel industry and its expansion has taken the Bowen name beyond its West Midlands base. The combined force of the Bowen Travel group is now around eighty coaches and over 40 travel agencies covering a geographical area that stretches from the West Midlands to the Lincolnshire Coast and to the counties of Northamptonshire and Buckinghamshire. The touring division carries around 75,000 people annually and the group travel divisions of Bowen Travel and Yorks Travel provide group organisers nationwide with travel and accommodation packages.

Recognition of the groups quality of service was endorsed in 2003 when Bowens were awarded the title of "Best large coach operator" by readers of "Group Travel Organiser" magazine and "Best Coach Operator – UK tours" by the readers of "Group Leisure" magazine.

Group Travel Organiser award for "Top large coach operator 2003".

Group Leisure award for "Best coach operator – UK Tours 2003".

Smethwick based Mann's Superlux Coaches was taken-over in November 1976.
WHA 440H, a Bedford VAL70 with Duple Viceroy 53-seat body was one of seven coaches acquired with the business. *B French collection*

EHA 600K was the newest of Mann's six Bedford VALs with Duple Viceroy body, and the only one to carry this striped version of their yellow and black livery. All of the former Mann's vehicles were sent to the Tamworth depot where they remained for a short time before being sold. *B French collection*

This general flyer from the late 1970's publicised all of the services available from the company.

A Pictorial History of the Bowen Coach Group

March 1977 - A half-page advertisement that appeared in the league cup final special edition of the "Sports Argus".

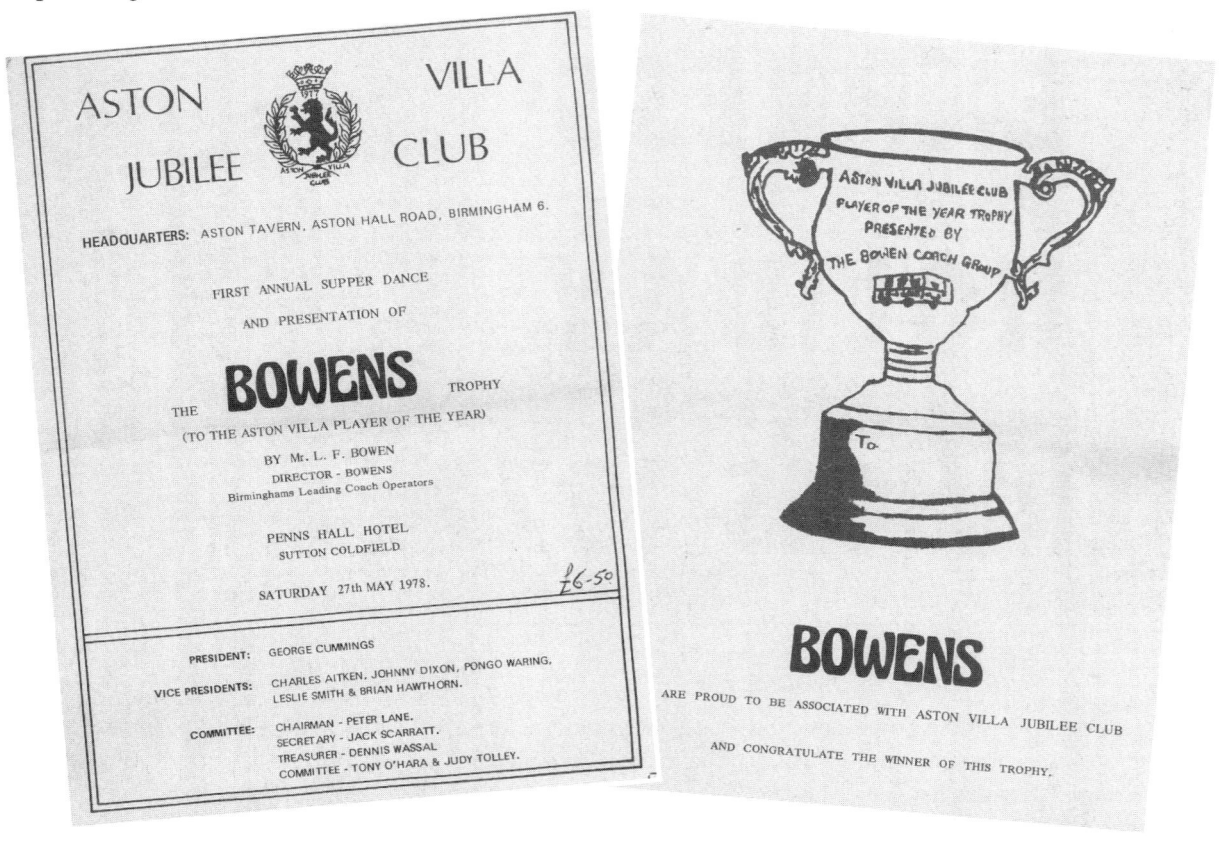

As well as providing coaches for the team and supporters, Bowens also sponsored the Aston Villa "Player of the Year" trophy. This souvenir programme is from the 1978 presentation that took place on May 27th.

BOWENS
EXPRESS HOLIDAY SERVICES 1977

EASTBOURNE SERVICE
(554 6375)
May 28th to September 24th

	a.m.
(Travel Bureau)	07.00
...doch Road	07.15
	07.21
	07.26
	07.33
	07.38
(...oad)	07.48
Arrive	13.30
Depart	14.00

£9.85, Children £4.95

CORTON-ON-SEA, ...ALL, HOPTON-ON-SEA, ...ESTOFT
(...4 6375)
...y 28th to September 24th

	06.45
	07.00
	07.14
ravel Bureau)	07.17
	07.23
	07.28
	07.31
	07.37
	07.42
	07.47
	08.00
...ad	08.05
	08.10
	07.15
	07.24
	07.15
	07.20
	07.26
	07.3.
	07.37
	07.45
	07.50
Arrive	13.30
Depart	14.00
Arrive	13.24
Depart	14.06
Arrive	13.18
Depart	14.12
Arrive	13.12
Depart	14.18
Arrive	13.09
Depart	14.21
Arrive	13.03
Depart	14.27

0, Children £4.55
5, Children £4.40
...issioner's Approval

A typical example of the brochures produced throughout the late 1970's and 1980's for the summer express services. These brochures usually had around 16-pages and featured over 30 express routes that operated on Saturdays between May and September. Pick-up points were available across the West Midlands area and on peak holiday weekends more than sixty coaches were deployed to take holidaymakers to their destinations. Many coaches were hired from other operators and a small selection of companies who regularly provided vehicles can be found on page 84.

1977 – PDA 285R Ford R1114 chassis with Caetano Estoril II 53-seat body, one of four identical coaches delivered in 1977. *P M Photography*

A nearside view of PDA 285R - these were the first vehicles to receive the revised livery of cream, dark red and yellow stripe. The fleet name was changed to simply "Bowens" and was applied in a new font style. *Photobus*

1977 – RUK 194R Ford A-series chassis with 25-seat Moseley Faro III body. Built by the Moseley Group in Loughborough, these small coaches were of a useful size but the Ford A-series was very noisy in operation. *PM Photography*

Part of the driving team from the late 1970's – from left to right: Unknown, Vic Sharlott, Clive Groves, Mick Kelly, John Wensley, John Barker, Ron Moseley, David Harrison, unknown. *J Wensley collection*

1978 – TOH 745S Bedford YMT chassis with 53-seat Van-Hool Mc.Ardle 300 body. A total of fifteen of these attractive coaches were acquired during late 1977 and early 1978. *A Roberts collection*

A nearside view of TOH 745S; the bodies for these coaches were built to Van-Hool's design under licence in Ireland by Mc.Ardle. This simplified version of the livery eventually became standard for the whole fleet.
A Roberts collection

1979 – YOX 508T Bedford YMT chassis with 53-seat Unicar Euro 80 GT body. This coach is pictured when new at the British Coach Rally where it was awarded the "Unicar Challenge" trophy. *PM Photography*

1979 – YOX 507T another Bedford YMT – Unicar, five of these were delivered to the fleet in 1979. The Unicar body was built in Spain and imported into the UK by Moseley's of Loughborough. Around eighty were sold on Bedford YMT chassis between 1979 and 1980, a further 18 were sold on Volvo B58 and a single example on a Ford R1114 chassis. *PM Photography*

This picture of Bedford – Unicar, YOX 509T, represents the batch after being re-painted into the new standard livery. All of the Unicar bodies purchased on Bedford chassis by Bowens were originally white, rather than cream, with a broad red and yellow band. *PM Photography*

1979 – YOX 505T Ford R1114 chassis with Duple Dominant II 53-seat body. This was the only example of the Dominant II body to be operated by the company. *Photobus*

Superior Coaches – The Bowen Story

"Going places with a smile"…this cheery little logo was used on brochures and publicity material in the late 1970's and early 1980's.

"Day Breaks" 1979 – each depot had its own edition of this day trip brochure.

1979 – XOJ 430 – 433T four new Bedford YMTs with Plaxton Supreme IV Express bodies, are pictured at the Plaxton factory in Scarborough prior to delivery. Sign writing and wheel trims had yet to be fitted.

1979 – XOJ 433T Bedford YMT chassis with 53-seat Plaxton Supreme IV Express body.
Daniel Hill photography

XOJ 432T, all four of these coaches were operated from the Tamworth depot where, amongst other duties, they were used on the stage registered colliery and works contracts – this enabled their purchase with the aid of the bus grant scheme. *PM Photography*

TGD 991R a Volvo B58 chassis with 53-seat Plaxton Viewmaster body which was originally new to Park's of Hamilton. This was one of a small number of coaches that operated from the short-lived London (East Grinstead) depot. *PM Photography*

RHP 8R a Volvo B58 chassis with Caetano Estoril II 53-seat body is another coach that was allocated to the East Grinstead operation. New in 1977 to Supreme Coaches of Coventry, this is the only example of this model of Caetano body that was operated by Bowens on a Volvo chassis. *Omnibus Society Collection*

1980 – EUK 546V one of two more Bedford YMTs with 53-seat Plaxton Supreme IV Express bodies for the Tamworth depot. *Photobus*

1980 – EOL 81V was one of two additional Unicar bodied Bedford YMTs to join the fleet. They were the last Bedford's purchased. *PM Photography*

1980 – EUK 548V Volvo B58 chassis with 53-seat Unicar Euro 80 GT body. This and EUK 549V were the last Unicar bodied coaches purchased, and the only examples on Volvo chassis. *A Roberts collection*

Both coaches had the red stripe over the yellow – the reverse order to the similarly bodied Bedford's in the fleet. *A Roberts collection*

When new, both of the Volvo – Unicars operated from the East Grinstead depot for a short time–hence the "Bowens, London" lettering on the boot door. *A Roberts collection*

An interior view of the EUK 549V, the Unicar body featured reclining seats, curtains, tinted windows and aisle carpet. The racks and roof lining were soft furnished rather than the formica finish of British bodies of the period. *A Roberts collection*

1981 – KJW 68W DAF MB200 chassis with Caetano Alpha GT 53-seat body. This was one of two new to the fleet in 1978 and is pictured at the British Coach Rally, Brighton. *Andrew Roberts*

KJW 69W was the second of the pair and in this picture is seen in the revised version of the livery that was later applied to these coaches. *Photobus*

1982 brochure of British and Continental holidays.

1982 – NOL 44X Volvo B58 chassis with Plaxton Supreme VI Express 51-seat body. This Plaxton model featured the unusual shallow side windows and was the only example of the type operated.

1982 – NOC 382X Ford R1114 chassis with 53-seat Caetano Alpha GT body – the last of many full-size Caetano bodies purchased by the company, it was also the last Ford chassis. *R H G Simpson*

The Bowens Darts Championships were held in Belgium throughout the 1980's and at the height of the series as many as twenty coaches carried contestants to the event from all over the UK. Some of the drivers involved with one of the tournaments are pictured here.

Terry Baller, Barry Blount, Ron Moseley, Ron Smallwood, Tony Morgan, Bill Smith, Dennis Hall, Brian Hastings, John Wensley, Dennis Hawthorn, George Jobson and Bill Hartin. *T Wright*

Some of the coaches pictured in Valkebburg *T Wright*

Back row: George Jobson, Dennis Hall, Dennis Bettaney
Front row: Unknown, Ron Smallwood, Brian Hastings and Roy Thomas
T Wright

Tony Wright, Ron Smallwood (known as Romel!), George Jobson, Dennis Hall and Brian Hastings
T Wright

Superior Coaches – The Bowen Story

ON HIRE TO BOWENS

"On hire to Bowens" Throughout the summer months the popularity of the express services operated by the company meant that additional coaches had to be hired from other operators. Over the years many companies were regular suppliers of coaches – some of the operators are no longer in business. Here is just a small selection of those who worked for Bowens on a regular basis.

Selandair of West Bromwich provided several coaches each summer weekend for many years. Here Plaxton Supreme IV bodied Ford R1114, VFK 661X is seen working coach number 2 on the Great Yarmouth service. Sealandair ceased operating in the early 1990's. *Photobus*

Lugg Valley Travel sent coaches from their base in Leominster, Herefordshire. TVJ 600S, a Bedford YMT with Duple Dominant II Express body represents their fleet. *PM Photography*

Another operator no longer in business, H & M Coaches were based in Chasetown. Representing their fleet is YFD 198X a Ford R1114 with Duple Dominant III body. *Photobus*

Plaxton Supreme bodied Bedford YMT, WSC 31R of G & G Coaches, Leamington Spa is pictured when operating a Bowen's Express Service at Lymington Road Coach Park in Torquay. G & G sold-out to Midland Red South - now part of the Stagecoach Group. *Photobus*

Harding's Coaches of Crabbs Cross near Redditch at one time supplied several vehicles each weekend. VWP 457M, an AEC Reliance with Plaxton Elite III Express body represents their fleet. *Andrew Roberts*

PSV 402, a Leyland Tiger with Jonckheere Jubilee P50 body from the Fillongley based L S Court fleet is pictured whilst working on hire to Bowens. *P M Photography*

84

1983 – TOC 884Y Bova Europa 53-seat integral. Two of these Dutch built coaches were acquired in 1983 and were the first of many Bovas to feature in the Bowens fleet in coming years. *A Roberts collection*

The Bova had a rear-mounted DAF engine and was imported by the Moseley Group. Air suspension was only just becoming commonplace on British operated coaches.

Another view of TOC 884Y, pictured whilst travelling on the M5 in July 1985. *J Mudge*

Superior Coaches – The Bowen Story

1984 summer season brochure: "Bowens the holidaymakers" logo introduced.

A separate brochure for autumn and spring holidays was published for the first time in 1984 under the "Breakaways" title. This series of brochures has been expanded over the years and also incorporates holidays for the festive period.

1984 – A865 XOP Bova Futura FHD 49-seat integral. Bova replaced their Europa model with the Futura range and more than twenty of this model was taken into the Bowen fleet over the next nine years. In this picture, the second version of the livery had been applied with the large sun and "the holidaymakers" logo.
A Roberts collection

Three Bova Futuras joined the fleet in 1984, of which two were of the low-floor FLD model – as represented here by A867 XOP which is seen in the original version of the livery applied to these vehicles.
A Roberts collection

1985 – B236 EOB Bova Futura FHD 49-seat integral, pictured at Torquay's Lymington Road coach park when operating on a Saturday express service. *A Roberts collection*

1985 – KJN 299 Volvo B10M chassis with 49-seat Van-Hool Alizee body. This coach was new in 1983 to Park's of Hamilton and was originally registered ODS 465Y. *Daniel Hill photography*

Bowens on tour…Bova Europa; TOC 884Y is pictured at Dartmouth – a popular excursion destination from one of the company's Torbay resort tours.

Bowens on tour…Tours of Scotland form an major part of the Bowen's holiday programme and here Bova Futura FHD, A865 XOP is pictured amidst the scenery of the "Rest and be thankful pass" near Arrochar.
T Mears

The small West Yorkshire business of Anderton's of Keighley was taken-over in 1985. Four Bedford YMT – Plaxton coaches, including XOJ 430T, were transferred to the operation to supplement its existing fleet. They retained Bowen's livery but with Anderton's fleet name. *A Roberts collection*

The Anderton operation was closed just over a year after its acquisition. A849 UGB was a DAF MB200 chassis with 49-seat Van-Hool Alizee body, originally from the Anderton fleet and retained by Bowens after Anderton's was closed. *Andrew Roberts*

1986 – EEW 125Y DAF SB2300 chassis with 49-seat Jonckheere Jubilee P599 body. This was one of seven coaches acquired from Nationwide of Lanark.
A Roberts collection

EEW 126Y, a second Jonckheere bodied DAF SB2300 ex-Nationwide, both coaches were originally new to Young's of Cambridge.
PM Photograph

All of the other coaches acquired from Nationwide were Plaxton bodied Volvo B58s, including EOI 4363 which had the high-floor Viewmaster IV body. New in 1979 as NFS 314T it is pictured when operating at the N.E.C.– note that the main fleet names have been removed; this was common at one time when coaches were retained for contract duties.
Daniel Hill photograph

Superior Coaches – The Bowen Story

1987 main season brochure for holidays in Britain, Ireland and the Continent.

A new series of brochures was launched for the first time in 1987 under the "Coastline Holidays" title. They featured packages to leading holiday centres and some hotels. Transportation was provided using the Bowens network of Saturday express services.

1987 – D230 POF Volvo B10M chassis with 49-seat Van-Hool Alizee body. The coach is pictured when new and whilst operating a tour to the Swiss resort of Lake Lugano. *T Mears*

Part of the driving team and office staff 1987, from left to right…
Back row; Frank Flynn, Maurice Jarvis.   Centre row; Derek Thompson, Brian Warren, Keith Aston, George Parker, Vic Sharlott, Bill Hartin, Pete Ramsall, Colin Rowe, John Jacques, Steve Robins, Barry Blount, George Frost, Terry Mears.   Front row; unknown, Pat…, Hilary Mears, Sharon…, Anne Warham. *T Mears*

Superior Coaches – The Bowen Story

Bowens on tour...Van-Hool bodied Volvo B10M, D230 POF is posed for the camera amidst snow-covered mountains in Switzerland.
T Mears

Bowens on tour...Stopping to admire the Swiss scenery.
T Mears

Bowens on tour...Time for photo-stop, en-route to Lugano.
T Mears

In 1987 Bowens were awarded the contract to operate the shuttle service between the car parks and exhibition halls at the National Exhibition Centre. Plaxton bodied Volvo B10M, E599 UHS is at the front of a line of coaches parked at the main entrance to the centre.

The contract was operated for eight years - during some of the busiest shows up to 30 vehicles were deployed each day. *Andrew Roberts*

Bowens on tour...Austria is one of the most popular European destinations in the Bowens holiday programme. In this view one of the companies Bova Futuras makes a stop amidst alpine scenery. *T Mears*

Bowens on tour...Another Austrian tour, Bova F31 COM takes a rest from the twisting ascent up one of the mountainous routes.
T Mears

Bowens on tour...Milan cathedral provides the backdrop of this picture of Volvo B10M – Van-Hool, D230 POF.
T Mears

1988 – D785 SGB Volvo B10M chassis with Plaxton Paramount III 3500 49-seat body, one of four identical 12-month old coaches to join the fleet from Park's of Hamilton. *A Roberts collection*

1988 – F30 COM, one of two new Bova Futura FHD 49-seat integrals delivered this year. Whilst outwardly similar, this and F31 COM differed from the other Bova Futuras in the fleet; although they had the same DAF engine an intercooler was fitted as well as the standard turbo-charger, this gave an additional 60 b.h.p. The seats were also arranged on a sloping floor, which meant that passengers at the back sat slightly higher than those at the front. Other differences included a power-operated continental exit door. *Andrew Roberts*

E599 UHS, a Volvo B10M with 49-seat Plaxton Paramount III 3500 body. This coach was acquired in 1990 from Ford's of Gunnislake in Cornwall, although it was new in 1988 to Park's of Hamilton. *Andrew Roberts*

Two used Bova Futura FHDs were also taken into the fleet in 1990 both were new in 1988 to Dance and Evans (Black Horse Travel) of London. E276 HRY is pictured outside Coventry cathedral on a private hire. *A Roberts collection*

"Breakaways" brochure for autumn 1990 / spring 1991.

1991 main season brochure; these were the first examples of a revised brochure design that featured a bold "Bowens" title on a white background. Future publications were of a similar design creating a familiar brand image.

1991 editions of the "pleasure days" and express holiday coach services brochures.

A Pictorial History of the Bowen Coach Group

Occasionally, a small number of contracted coaches, in Bowens livery, are used for the coach holiday programme. YWH 978 is a Van-Hool bodied Volvo B10M that was operated by Bowers Coaches of Chapel-en-le-Frith. *Daniel Hill photography*

Keith's Coaches of Blucher, Tyne and Wear provided OCM 937, a Leyland Tiger with Van-Hool Alizee body. It is pictured whilst operating at the NEC on the car park shuttle service. *Daniel Hill photography*

1991 – H621 FUT, one of three more new Bova FHD Futuras for the fleet. All three were required in service immediately upon delivery before the full livery had been applied. They were operated for their first season in plain cream with just the sun logo and fleet names.

A rear view of H621 FUT, the "FUT" in the registration was a reference to the "Futura" model name – this was a feature of a number of Bovas supplied in 1991 by Moseley's of Loughborough.

This picture of H619 FUT represents the 1991 Bovas after full livery has been applied – "The Holiday Makers" title was replaced with "The first choice for holidays" legend. *Andrew Roberts*

1992 – J407 AWF one of three more Bova FHD integrals. These were the first coaches purchased with full air-conditioning; this equipment was subsequently standard for all new fleet acquisitions. *Andrew Roberts*

To promote the 1993 holiday programme, the services of comedian Jim Bowen were engaged.

Jim appeared in the brochure, press advertising and the Bowen Travel agencies even displayed life-size cardboard Jim Bowens!

At the time Jim Bowen hosted the popular darts based show "Bulls eye" and his catchphrase of "super, smashing, great" was played upon in advertising.

A Pictorial History of the Bowen Coach Group

Jim Bowen briefs drivers Frank Flynn, John Edgington, Derek Thompson, George Parker, unknown, unknown and Bob Melville.

BOWENS 1993 EXPRESS COACH HOLIDAY SERVICES

1993 FARES AT 1991 PRICES

NEW FOR 1993
EXPRESS COACHES ARE NOW NO SMOKING

SUMMER SATURDAY COACH SERVICES TO OVER 50 OF THE UK's PREMIER SEASIDE RESORTS

TELEPHONE 021-327 3205 (4 LINES)

BOWENS PLEASURE DAYS 1993

NO COACH FARE INCREASES FOR 1993
NEW FOR 1993 Pleasure day coaches are now no smoking

FOR ALL ENQUIRIES RING 021-327 5921
L.F. BOWEN LTD.
101 Cotterills Lane, Alum Rock
Birmingham B8 3SA

1993 brochures for summer express services and pleasure days – note that the fares for 1993 were the same as 1991! Also all coaches were now non-smoking.

1993 – A further four Bova Futura FHDs were added to the fleet. Two of the batch; K296 GDT and K 297 GDT are pictured here in front of Shugborough Hall in Staffordshire.

1993 – K714 RNR Toyota Coaster chassis with 18-seat Caetano Optimo II body. Two of these coaches joined the fleet in 1993. *Andrew Roberts*

A Pictorial History of the Bowen Coach Group

1994 – After purchasing many Dutch built Bovas, a change in policy saw four Scania K113 chassis with Spanish built Irizar Century bodies enter the fleet. L408 LHE is pictured when new at the M.I.R.A. test track near Nuneaton. This coach was featured in the advertisements of Scania UK in the trade publications of the time.

Bowens on tour…An Irizar bodied Scania is pictured, during a Scottish tour, by Eileen Donan Castle on Loch Duich. *T Mears*

Bowens on tour…Another Scania – Irizar rests in the Scottish sunshine with Ben Nevis in the background. *T Mears*

1995 – A further four Irizar Century bodied Scania K113s joined the fleet. M319 VET is pictured at the National Exhibition Centre.

A rear view of M319 VET – the symbols on the back window refer to the equipment on the vehicle - ABS braking system, Air-conditioning, Reclining seats, Audio system, individual lights, TV / Video, W.C., drinks.
Andrew Roberts

1995 main season and "Breakaways" 1995 / 1996 brochures.

An example of one of the brochures published by the Group Travel Division; this featured suggested packages and itineraries for group travel organisers and coach operators.

1996 – N815DKU Scania K113 chassis with Irizar Century 49-seat body, one of five purchased for the 1996 season. *PM Photography*

N811 DKU, another of the 1996 intake of Scanias is pictured whilst operating a UK tour on behalf of the Bowens European Incoming Groups Division. It is seen at Warwick Castle awaiting the return of its American tour group. *Andrew Roberts*

Superior Coaches – The Bowen Story

1998 Express services and pleasure days brochures.

Below, an example of one of the brochures published by the European Incoming Tours Division; this featured a range of European tour itineraries for the North American market. The brochures were distributed at trade fairs and to travel agents in the USA.

Two more Scania K113 with Irizar Century bodies joined the fleet in 1997. One of the two, P194 GHE is pictured whilst on tour in Scotland at the Rotheimurchus Highland Estate. *T Mears*

Bowens were one of the largest fleet customers for the Scania – Irizar combination, with 15 purchased new between 1994 and 1997. Former Bowen's chairman, Jim Ball and Don MacIntosh of Scania UK are pictured with eleven representatives of the type from the Bowen fleet.

Superior Coaches – The Bowen Story

The long established business of York's of Northampton was taken-over including its fleet of around 30 coaches in September 1997.

The York's fleet included many examples of the German Kassbohrer Setra; VHM 847 represents the high floor S215HD model. The coach was new in 1991 to Ball, Folkestone and was originally registered F992 MTW.
Andrew Roberts

From 1946 most coaches in the York's fleet were named after Royal Naval ships, as seen here by Kassbohrer Setras ERV 324 "HMS Gloucester" and VHM 847 "HMS Ark Royal". Fleet numbers are also employed on all York's vehicles.
Andrew Roberts

The York's fleet also included a number of Volvo B10M based coaches; UFC 221 is a B10M with 53-seat Plaxton Paramount III 3500 body. Originally registered E70 LVV it was new to the company in 1988 and is named "HMS Torbay". *Andrew Roberts*

A Pictorial History of the Bowen Coach Group

York's ESK 896, a Volvo B10M with 53-seat Van-Hool Alizee body. Allocated fleet number 52 and named "HMS Conqueror", this coach was originally registered D610 MVR and was acquired by York's in 1992 from Shearings. *Andrew Roberts*

TVY 659 is an example of the low floor Kassbohrer Setra S215HR "Rationale" model. Named "HMS Beaver" this coach was new to York's in 1986 and was originally registered C98 RVV. This was one of a small number of coaches painted in this version of the York's livery which had a silver-blue base with two blue, and one red, stripes applied in a similar fashion to the London based Travellers Coach Company fleet. *Andrew Roberts*

York's Kassbohrer Setra S215HD, 846 FHA was one of a few vehicles to receive full Bowen's livery. York's programme of holidays was incorporated into the Bowens brochure with York's providing some vehicles for the combined programme. 846 FHA was new in 1993 to Spirit of London Coaches and is named "HMS Iron Duke". *Andrew Roberts*

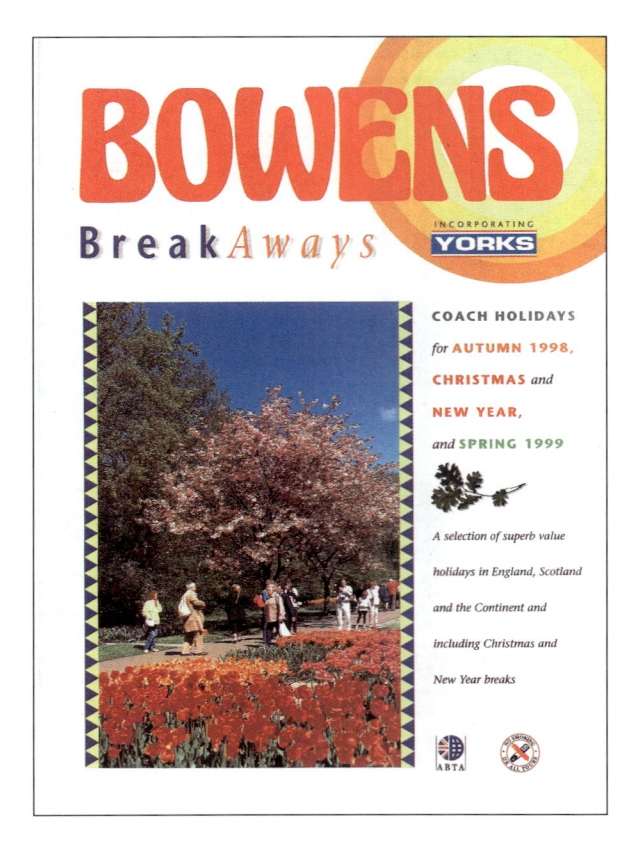

The brochures published for autumn 1998 / spring 1999, and main season 1999 were the first to incorporate the Yorks name on the front cover.

A Pictorial History of the Bowen Coach Group

1998 – R645 VNN M.A.N. 18-310 chassis with Noge Catalan 3.50 49-seat body, pictured when new at the UK Coach Rally, Brighton. *Andrew Roberts*

The M.A.N. – Noge combination introduced a new type to the fleet; three each for Bowens and Yorks were acquired in 1998. They were the last new coaches to be delivered in the traditional cream and red livery – they were also the only vehicles to have the fleet name applied to the front windscreen. *Andrew Roberts*

R637 VNN, another of the 1998 M.A.N. – Noge intake for the Bowen fleet. The Noge body was built in Arbucies, Spain and imported into the UK by Alf Moseley Continental, parent company to the Bowen group. In other parts of Europe the model is known as the "Touring" and it was voted "Coach of the Year, 1996" in Spain.

R636 VNN represents one of the York's fleet allocation with fleet number 71 it was christened "HMS Vengeance". *PM Photography*

1999 – A new common livery for the Bowens and Yorks fleet was introduced. The first coaches to appear in this silver-based scheme were the 1998 Noge bodied M.A.N.s. R633 VNN demonstrates the Bowen version.

R638 VNN, "HMS Vigilant" from the Yorks fleet showed off the new livery at the UK Coach Rally, Brighton in April 1999. *Andrew Roberts*

1999 – Two more Noge Catalan bodied M.A.N. 18.310s were delivered to the Bowen fleet. T194 SUT is pictured at the UK Coach Rally, Brighton in April 2000. *Andrew Roberts*

A rear view of T194 SUT shows the back of the Noge body and the Bowen livery application. *Andrew Roberts*

1999 – T183 SUT M.A.N. 24.400 chassis with Marcopolo Continental 360 49-seat body. This coach represented the Yorks fleet at the UK Coach Rally in April 2000. *Andrew Roberts*

A rear view of T183 SUT - The Marcopolo body was built in Portugal and was another offering from Alf Moseley Continental. This was the first example imported on the tri-axle M.A.N. chassis. *Andrew Roberts*

Superior Coaches – The Bowen Story

N566 AWJ – Neoplan N316SHD Cityliner; this coach joined the Bowen fleet in 1999 from Parry's of Cheslyn Hay. *Andrew Roberts*

The impressive looking Neoplan was equipped with a galley kitchen and full "executive" facilities. The coach was mainly used on high-class corporate charter work and was usually fitted with 32-seats and four tables. *Andrew Roberts*

2000 – W752 AAY M.A.N. 18.350 chassis with 49-seat Marcopolo Continental 340 body; one of two for the Bowen fleet. *Andrew Roberts*

These coaches were the first for the fleet with an automatic gearbox. *Andrew Roberts*

2000 – W822 BOM Toyota Coaster chassis with Caetano Optimo III body; one of two delivered to the Bowen fleet, both were of the wider version of the Optimo body allowing 22 seats. *Andrew Roberts*

2000 – W751 AAY M.A.N. 24.400 chassis with 49-seat Marcopolo Continental 360 body - the second of the type to be placed into the Yorks fleet. *Andrew Roberts*

The coach touring division of Appleby's of Louth in Lincolnshire was taken-over in November 2000. Fourteen coaches and a number of travel agencies were included in the deal. The Appleby's "Super Coach Holidays" brochure continues separate from the Bowens programme and, to-date, the cream and green livery has been retained.

All of the coaches acquired with the Appleby's business were of the Scania – Irizar combination, a mixture of two and three axle versions. N356 REE represents the Scania K113CRTB chassis with the higher 3.7 metre high version of the Irizar Century body. *Andrew Roberts*

Appleby's T849 JFU has the Scania K124IB4 two axle chassis fitted with the later version of the Irizar Century body. All of the Appleby vehicles have the "Royal Class" logo. *Andrew Roberts*

2001 – Yorks Y664 NAY M.A.N. 24.400 chassis with 49-seat Marcopolo Continental 360 body. It is pictured at the 2001 UK Coach Rally in Brighton where it received the top placed Marcopolo award. *Andrew Roberts*

Bowens M.A.N. 18.310 – Noge Catalan, T193 SUT also represented the company at the 2001 UK Coach Rally and was awarded the trophy for the highest placed Noge. *Andrew Roberts*

2001 – All of the remaining Bova Futuras were re-painted into the new silver colour scheme. The four 1993 examples also received a full interior refurbishment. K296 GDT is pictured shortly after completion.
Andrew Roberts

An off-side view of K296 GDT, the new livery up-dated the appearance of these vehicles.
Andrew Roberts

Many of the York's fleet have also been re-painted, as seen by FSV 305, "HMS Trafalgar" a Kassbohrer Setra S215HR. *Andrew Roberts*

One York's coach currently in non-standard livery is S604 VAY, a high floor example of the Noge Catalan on three-axle M.A.N. 24.400 chassis. Originally owned by Coachstop of Leigh-on-sea; the "Chief" livery was typical of their vehicles, all of which had specially commissioned airbrush paint schemes.
Andrew Roberts

2002 – FN 02 HGX Dennis Javelin chassis with 48-seat Marcopolo Continental 340 body; one of three identical vehicles delivered to the Yorks, Northampton fleet. *Andrew Roberts*

These three coaches were amongst the last from the stock of Alf Moseley Continental before the Marcopolo franchise was transferred to B.A.S.E. of Ormskirk. Their delivery also re-introduced the Dennis chassis to a Bowen group fleet – the last examples being the Lancet IIIs of 1950. *Andrew Roberts*

2002 – Four more M.A.N. 18.310 chassis with 49-seat Noge Catalan bodies were added to the Bowen fleet. FN 02 HGK is pictured in the sunshine at Brighton when just a few weeks old. *Andrew Roberts*

FN 02 HGM, another of the quintet is pictured whilst on tour in the French Alps. These four coaches were amongst the last supplied by Alf Moseley. The Noge franchise was transferred to Neoplan UK – later known as Mentor. *T Mears*

At the end of 2003 the only coaches remaining in the cream and red livery were the Irizar bodied Scanias. P194 GHE was one of the first to be re-painted into the silver scheme in December 2003. *Andrew Roberts*

This rear view of P194 GHE shows the new image. Further examples were re-painted in early 2004. *Andrew Roberts*

"Bowen House", the new operations centre on the Lichfield Road Industrial Estate in Tamworth. *Andrew Roberts*

The centre has a modern three-bay maintenance building. *Andrew Roberts*

The site was formerly occupied by the Territorial Army and has a spacious office block. *Andrew Roberts*

Additional adjacent land was also acquired to provide a large coach parking area. *Andrew Roberts*

Scania – Irizar, N815 DKU is taken through the new Britannia wash. *Andrew Roberts*

A Pictorial History of the Bowen Coach Group

One of the 1965 Harrington Grenadier bodied AEC Reliances; BOF 859C has managed to escape the breaker's yard and is currently undergoing restoration by its owner, Phil Roberts (no relation to Andrew Roberts!).

The coach was new to L F Bowen in March 1965 and was operated until January 1972. Lamb's Coaches of Malton in Yorkshire became the second owners and it is believed that the coach spent the rest of its operating life in the North of England. The present owner acquired it in late 1990 from someone in Hexham.

Another of the batch, BOF 858C, is believed to survive in Lydney, Gloucestershire – although this coach has unfortunately been converted into a stock-car transporter and is now in a derelict condition.

Most of the work carried out to-date has involved repairing the mechanics, including fitting a new AEC 550 engine – in place of the original 470 unit.

Work will start in the spring of 2004 on renovating the bodywork and, although a lot of work is required – both outside and inside, it is hoped that BOF 859C will be restored to its former glory (in L F Bowen "Superior Coaches" livery) within the next two years.
All pictures – Andrew Roberts

L F BOWEN - Fleet List

Year Acquired	Reg No.	Chassis	Bodywork	Seats	Year New	Notes
?	VO 652	Gilford 1680T	?	B32	1929	Ex Watts & Bury, Reddington
1939	VC 1800	Daimler CF6	Buckingham	C32	1929	Ex Stilgoe, Birmingham
1939	FV 49	Leyland TS1	?	C29R	1929	" " " "
1939	GF 483	AEC Regal	Hoyal	C32F	1930	" " " "
1939	VS 2095	AEC Regal	Harrington	C30	1931	" " " "
1939	BOM 311	Dennis Lancet I	?	C32F	1936	" " " "
1941	EHA 450	Dennis Lancet II	Auto-Cellulose	C32F	1938	Ex Ashmore, Smethwick
1941	AUY 154	Dennis Lancet II	Dennis	C32C	1936	Ex Clarke, Rubery
1943	FON 854	Maudslay ML3F	Harrington	C32F	1943	Ex War Dept (a)
1943	FON 855	Maudslay ML4	?	?	1943	Ex War Dept (b)
1943	CK 4745	Leyland TS6	English Electric	C32R	1933	Ex War Dept (ex Ribble 1391)
1943	FON 881	Bedford WTB	Duple	C25F	1943	Ex War Dept (c)
1946	EOG 710	Bedford WTB	Holbrook	C26F	1938	Ex Hunter, Birmingham
1946	BTE 893	Dennis Lancet I	Duple	C32	1937	Ex Dean, Manchester
1946	CNF 346	Leyland LT7	?	C32F	1936	Ex Hunt, Bickerstaffe
1946	GOJ 424	Dennis Lancet	Santus	C33F	1946	
1947	GOP 868	Maudslay Marathon 3	Santus	C33F	1947	
1947	GOV 657	Dennis Lancet III	Santus	C33F	1947	
1947	GOV 658	" "	"	C33F	1947	
1947	HOH 431	" "	"	C33F	1947	
1948	HOM 917	Maudslay Marathon 3	Santus	C33F	1948	
1948	HOP 749	Dennis Lancet III	Santus	C33F	1948	
1948	HOV 426	Dennis Lance	Santus	C33F	1948	
1949	JOL 375	Maudslay Marathon	Santus	C33F	1949	
1949	JOH 946	Seddon P6 Mk IV	Santus	C31F	1949	
1950	KOE 478	Dennis Lancet III	Santus	FC33F	1950	
1950	KOB 748	" "	"	FC33F	1950	
1950	KOC 668	" "	"	FC33F	1950	
1950	KOE 794	" "	"	FC33F	1950	
1950	KOF 229	" "	"	FC33F	1950	
1952	LOX 427	AEC Regal IV	Burlingham Seagull	C37C	1952	
1953	NOF 550	" "	" "	C37F	1953	
1956	TOB 334	Bedford SBG	Burlingham Seagull	C41F	1956	
1956	TOB 335	" "	" "	C41F	1956	
1956	TOB 336	" "	" "	C41F	1956	
1957	UOE 30	" "	" "	C41F	1957	
1957	UOE 31	" "	" "	C41F	1957	
1957	UOE 32	" "	" "	C41F	1957	
1957	UOE 33	" "	" "	C41F	1957	
1957	UOE 34	" "	" "	C41F	1957	
1958	ROX 184	AEC Reliance MU3RV	Burlingham Seagull	C41C	1955	Ex Winwood, Birmingham
1958	TOX 939	Bedford SBG	Duple Vega	C41F	1956	" " "
1958	WOV 652	Bedford SB3	Duple Vega	C41F	1958	
1958	WOV 653	" "	" "	C41F	1958	
1958	XOJ 606	Bedford SB3	Duple Super Vega	C41F	1958	
1959	XOJ 607	" "	" "	C41F	1959	
1959	XOJ 608	" "	" "	C41F	1959	
1959	XOJ 609	" "	" "	C41F	1959	
1959	XOJ 610	" "	" "	C41F	1959	
1959	XOV 690	" "	" "	C41F	1959	
1959	2155 VP	AEC Reliance 2MU3RA	Plaxton Panorama	C41F	1959	
1961	793 COE	Bedford SB8	Harrington Crusader II	C41F	1961	
1961	794 COE	" "	" "	C41F	1961	
1961	795 COE	" "	" "	C41F	1961	
1961	796 COE	" "	" "	C41F	1961	
1961	797 COE	" "	" "	C41F	1961	
1961	798 COE	" "	" "	C41F	1961	
1961	799 COE	" "	" "	C41F	1961	
1963	906 HOX	Bedford SB5	Harrington Crusader III	C41F	1963	
1963	794 JOB	AEC Reliance 2U3RA	Plaxton Panorama	C51F	1963	
1964	80 JPF	Bedford SB1	Burlingham Seagull	C41F	1959	Ex Richmond, Epsom
1964	495 KPC	" "	" "	C41F	1959	" " "
1965	BOF 854C	AEC Reliance 2U3RA	Harrington Grenadier	C51F	1965	
1965	BOF 855C	" "	" "	C51F	1965	
1965	BOF 856C	" "	" "	C51F	1965	
1965	BOF 857C	AEC Reliance 2MU4RA	Harrington Grenadier	C41F	1965	
1965	BOF 858C	" "	" "	C41F	1965	
1965	BOF 859C	" "	" "	C41F	1965	
1966	FOF 438D	AEC Reliance 2U3RA	Plaxton Panorama I	C49F	1966	
1966	FOM 807D	Bedford VAS1	Plaxton Panorama I	C29F	1966	
1966	GOH 494D	AEC Reliance 2U3RA	Plaxton Panorama I	C51F	1966	
1966	917 GOF	Bedford SB8	Duple Super Vega	C41F	1962	Ex Newton, Birmingham
1967	JOE 189E	AEC Reliance 2U3RA	Plaxton Panorama I	C51F	1967	
1968	NMB 301D	Bedford VAL14	Plaxton Panorama I	C52F	1966	Ex Jackson, Altricham
1968	NMB 305D	" "	" "	C52F	1966	" " "
1968	LOV 761F	AEC Reliance 6U3ZR	Plaxton Panorama I	C51F	1968	

134

L F BOWEN - Fleet List

Year Acquired	Reg No.	Chassis	Bodywork	Seats	Year New	Notes
1968	EOT 721D	Bedford VAL14	Plaxton Panorama I	C52F	1966	Ex Arnold, Tamworth
1969	POC 827G	Bedford VAL70	Plaxton Panorama Elite	C53F	1969	
1969	ROA 728G	AEC Reliance 6U3ZR	Plaxton Panorama Elite	C51F	1969	L F Bowen (Small Heath) Ltd
1969	ROA 729G	" " "	" "	C51F	1969	
1969	ROA 730G	" " "	" "	C51F	1969	
1969	ROA 731G	" " "	" "	C51F	1969	
1969	6911 HA	Leyland PSU3/3R	Harrington Grenadier	C49F	1963	Ex Gliderways, Smethwick
1969	6912 HA	" "	" "	C49F	1963	" " " "
1969	8757 HA	Leyland Leopard PSU3/3RT	Harrington Grenadier	C51F	1964	" " " "
1969	8758 HA	" "	" "	C51F	1964	" " " "
1969	FHA 903D	Leyland Leopard PSU3/3RT	Plaxton Panorama I	C49F	1966	" " " "
1969	FHA 904D	" "	" "	C49F	1966	" " " "
1970	SOL 832H	AEC Reliance 6U3ZR	Caetano Lisboa	C51F	1970	
1970	JEF 94G	Bedford VAM70	Plaxton Panorama Elite	C45F	1969	Ex Richardson, Hartlepool
1970	BMA 903F	Bedford VAL70	Plaxton Panorama I	C53F	1968	Ex Bullock, Cheadale
1970	UOH 634H	AEC Reliance 6U3ZR	Caetano Lisboa	C51F	1970	
1970	UOH 635H	" "	" "	C51F	1970	
1971	WVP 704J	AEC Reliance 6MU4R	Caetano Lisboa	C51F	1971	
1971	WVP 705J	" "	" "	C51F	1971	
1971	XOH 70J	Ford R226	Caetano Estoril	C53F	1971	
1971	XOH 71J	" "	" "	C53F	1971	
1971	XOH 72J	" "	" "	C53F	1971	
1971	XOH 73J	" "	" "	C53F	1971	
1971	YOH 849J	Bedford YRQ	Duple Viceroy	C45F	1971	
1971	YOH 850J	" "	" "	C45F	1971	
1971	YOJ 21J	" "	" "	C45F	1971	
1971	YOJ 22J	" "	" "	C45F	1971	
1971	YOA 693J	" "	" "	C45F	1971	
1971	YOA 694J	" "	" "	C45F	1971	
1971	YOJ 227J	" "	" "	C45F	1971	
1971	AOH 561K	U.T.I.C. – AEC	Utic Tagus	C53F	1971	
1971	AOM 14K	Ford R226	Caetano Estoril	C53F	1971	
1971	AOM 15K	" "	" "	C53F	1971	
1971	AOM 16K	" "	" "	C53F	1971	
1971	AOM 17K	" "	" "	C53F	1971	
1972	BOA 943K	AEC Reliance 6U3ZR	Caetano Lisboa	C51F	1972	
1972	BOA 944K	" "	" "	C51F	1972	
1972	BOA 945K	" "	" "	C51F	1972	
1972	BOA 946K	" "	" "	C51F	1972	
1972	COA 748K	" "	" "	C57F	1972	
1972	COA 749K	" "	" "	C57F	1972	
1972	COG 32K	Bedford YRQ	Caetano Cascais	C45F	1972	
1972	COG 34K	" "	" "	C45F	1972	
1972	COG 35K	" "	" "	C45F	1972	
1972	COG 36K	" "	" "	C45F	1972	
1972	COG 37K	" "	" "	C45F	1972	
1972	COG 38K	" "	" "	C45F	1972	
1972	CON 280K	" "	" "	C45F	1972	
1972	CON 281K	" "	" "	C45F	1972	
1972	CON 282K	" "	" "	C45F	1972	
1972	DOV 948K	Ford Transit	Moseley	12	1972	
1972	FOK 824L	Bedford YRT	Caetano Estoril II	C40F	1972	
1973	FDH 707H	Leyland Leopard PSU3A/4RT	Caetano Lisboa	C40F	1970	Ex Walsall Coach and Travel
1973	LDH 808J	Seddon Pennine IV	Caetano Estoril	C46F	1971	" " " " "
1973	UDH 10K	Ford Transit	Moseley	12	1972	" " " " "
1973	GOK 957L	Bedford YRT	Caetano Estoril II	C53F	1973	
1973	GOK 958L	" "	" "	C53F	1973	
1973	HOM 466L	" "	" "	C53F	1973	
1973	HOM 467L	" "	" "	C53F	1973	
1973	HOM 468L	" "	" "	C53F	1973	
1973	HOM 469L	" "	" "	C53F	1973	
1973	HOM 470L	" "	" "	C53F	1973	
1973	HOM 471L	" "	" "	C40F	1973	
1973	HOM 472L	" "	" "	C53F	1973	
1973	HOM 473L	" "	" "	C53F	1973	
1974	GDU 66L	U.T.I.C. – AEC	Utic Tagus	C53F	1972	Ex Supreme (Bonas), Coventry
1974	GHP 994L	" "	" "	C53F	1973	" " " "
1975	JUK 948N	Leyland Leopard PSU3B/4R	Plaxton Panorama Elite III	C53F	1975	
1975	JUK 949N	" "	" " "	C53F	1975	
1975	JUK 950N	" "	" " "	C53F	1975	
1975	KOG 947P	Leyland Leopard PSU3C/4R	Plaxton Panorama Elite III	C34F	1975	
1975	LUK 9P	AEC Reliance 6U3ZR	Plaxton Supreme	C53F	1975	later re-registered UPF 807
1975	LUK 10P	AEC Reliance 6U3ZR	Plaxton Panorama Elite III	C53F	1975	
1975	LUK 82P	Ford R1114	Duple Dominant	C53F	1975	
1975	LUK 83P	" "	" "	C53F	1975	
1975	LUK 84P	" "	" "	C53F	1975	

L F BOWEN - Fleet List

Year Acquired	Reg No.	Chassis	Bodywork	Seats	Year New	Notes
1975	LUK 85P	Ford R1114	Duple Dominant	C53F	1975	
1975	LUK 86P	" "	" "	C53F	1975	
1975	LUK 87P	" "	" "	C53F	1975	
1976	LXE 886K	Ford R226	Duple Viceroy	C53F	1972	Ex Welwyn Garden City, St.Albans
1976	SDH 101K	" "	" "	C53F	1972	Ex Central, Walsall
1976	SDH 102K	" "	" "	C53F	1972	" " "
1976	THA 209G	Bedford VAL70	Duple Viceroy	C53F	1969	(AD) Ex Mann, Smethwick
1976	THA 210G	" "	" "	C53F	1969	(AD) " " "
1976	WHA 440H	" "	" "	C53F	1970	(AD) " " "
1976	AHA 667J	" "	" "	C53F	1971	(AD) " " "
1976	AHA 668J	" "	" "	C53F	1971	(AD) " " "
1976	EHA 600K	" "	" "	C53F	1972	(AD) " " "
1976	KHA 341L	Bedford YRT	Duple Dominant	C53F	1973	(AD) " " "
1977	HRU 703N	Ford R1114	Plaxton Panorama Elite III	C49F	1975	Ex A.C., Bournemouth
1977	HRU 705N	" "	" "	C49F	1975	" " "
1977	RUK 194R	Ford A0609	Moseley Faro	C25F	1977	
1977	PDA 282R	Ford R1114	Caetano Estoril II	C53F	1977	(AD)
1977	PDA 283R	" "	" "	C53F	1977	(AD)
1977	PDA 284R	" "	" "	C53F	1977	(AD)
1977	PDA 285R	" "	" "	C53F	1977	(AD)
1977	TOH 732S	Bedford YMT	Van-Hool Mc.Ardle 300	C53F	1977	
1977	TOH 733S	" "	" " "	C53F	1977	
1977	TOH 734S	" "	" " "	C53F	1977	
1977	TOH 735S	" "	" " "	C53F	1977	
1977	TOH 736S	" "	" " "	C53F	1977	
1978	TOH 737S	" "	" " "	C53F	1978	
1978	TOH 738S	" "	" " "	C53F	1978	
1978	TOH 739S	" "	" " "	C53F	1978	
1978	TOH 740S	" "	" " "	C53F	1978	
1978	TOH 741S	" "	" " "	C53F	1978	
1978	TOH 742S	" "	" " "	C53F	1978	
1978	TOH 743S	" "	" " "	C53F	1978	
1978	TOH 744S	" "	" " "	C53F	1978	
1978	TOH 745S	" "	" " "	C53F	1978	
1978	TOH 746S	" "	" " "	C53F	1978	(AD)
1978	TOH 747S	" "	" " "	C53F	1978	(AD)
1978	KVP 939P	Ford R1114	Duple Dominant	C53F	1975	Ex Park, Hamilton
1978	KVP 940P	" "	" "	C53F	1975	" " "
1979	XOJ 430T	Bedford YMT	Plaxton Supreme IV Express	C53F	1979	(AD)
1979	XOJ 431T	" "	" "	C53F	1979	(AD)
1979	XOJ 432T	" "	" "	C53F	1979	(AD)
1979	XOJ 433T	" "	" "	C53F	1979	(AD)
1979	YOX 505T	Ford R1114	Duple Dominant II	C53F	1979	
1979	YOX 506T	Bedford YMT	Unicar Euro 80 GT	C53F	1979	
1979	YOX 507T	" "	" "	C53F	1979	
1979	YOX 508T	" "	" "	C53F	1979	
1979	YOX 509T	" "	" "	C53F	1979	
1979	YOX 510T	" "	" "	C53F	1979	
1980	EUK 546V	Bedford YMT	Plaxton Supreme IV Express	C53F	1980	(A)
1980	EUK 547V	" "	" "	C53F	1980	(A)
1980	EUK 548V	Volvo B58-61	Unicar Euro 80 GT	C53F	1980	later re-registered EOI 4362
1980	EUK 549V	" "	" "	C53F	1980	later re-registered UFA 756
1980	EOL 81V	Bedford YMT	Unicar Euro 80 GT	C53F	1980	
1980	EOL 82V	" "	" "	C53F	1980	
1981	GOV 573W	Ford A0609	Moseley Faro	C21F	1981	
1981	KJW 68W	DAF MB200	Caetano Alpha GT	C53F	1981	
1981	KJW 69W	" "	" "	C53F	1981	
1982	NOC 382X	Ford R1114	Caetano Alpha GT	C49F	1982	(AD)
1982	NOL 44X	Volvo B58-56	Plaxton Supreme VI Express	C51F	1982	(AD)
1983	TOC 884Y	Bova EL26	Bova Europa	C53F	1983	(AD)
1983	TOC 885Y	" "	" "	C53F	1983	(AD)
1984	A865 XOP	Bova 12-280	Bova Futura FHD	C49FT	1984	(AD)
1984	A866 XOP	Bova 12-250	Bova Futura FLD	C49F	1984	(AD)
1984	A867 XOP	" "	" "	C49F	1984	(AD)
1985	B236 EOB	Bova 12-280	Bova Futura FHD	C49FT	1985	(AD)
1985	B237 EOB	" "	" "	C49FT	1985	(AD)
1985	KJN 299	Volvo B10M	Van-Hool Alizee	C49FT	1983	(AD) Ex Park Hamilton
1985	A849 UGB	DAF MB200	Van-Hool Alizee	C49FT	1984	(AD) Ex Anderton, Keighley
1986	TAC 253W	Volvo B58	Plaxton Supreme IV	C57F	1981	(AD) Ex Nationwide, Lanark
1986	EEW 125Y	DAF SB2300	Jonckheere Jubilee P599	C51FT	1983	(AD) " " "
1986	EEW 126Y	" "	" "	C51FT	1983	(AD) " " "
1986	12 DLY	Volvo B58	Plaxton Viewmaster IV	C50F	1983	(AD) " " " (e)
1986	9712 WX	" "	" "	C50F	1983	(AD) " " " (f)
1986	NFS 314T	" "	" "	C50F	1979	(AD) " " " (g)
1986	NFS 373T	" "	" "	C50F	1979	(AD) " " " (h)

L F BOWEN - Fleet List

Year Acquired	Reg No.	Chassis	Bodywork	Seats	Year New	Notes
1987	D230 POF	Volvo B10M	Van-Hool Alizee	C53F	1987	(AD)
1987	D231 POF	Bova 12-280	Bova Futura FHD	C53F	1987	(AD)
1987	D424 POF	" "	" " "	C53F	1987	(AD)
1988	D784 SGB	Volvo B10M	Plaxton Paramount III 3500	C49FT	1987	Ex Park, Hamilton
1988	D785 SGB	" "	" " "	C49FT	1987	" " "
1988	D786 SGB	" "	" " "	C49FT	1987	" " "
1988	D787 SGB	" "	" " "	C49FT	1987	" " "
1989	F 30 COM	Bova 12-360	Bova Futura FHD	C53F	1989	
1989	F 31 COM	" "	" " "	C53F	1989	
1989	F696 ONR	Bova 12-290	Bova Futura FHD	C53F	1988	Ex Moseley demonstrator
1990	E276 HRY	" "	" " "	C53F	1988	Ex Dance and Evans, London
1990	E673 JNR	" "	" " "	C49FT	1988	" " " "
1990	E599 UHS	Volvo B10M	Plaxton Paramount III 3500	C51F	1988	Ex Ford, Gunnislake
1990	E274 HRY	" "	" " "	C51F	1988	Ex Smith, Murton
1991	H619 FUT	Bova 12-290	Bova Futura FHD	C49FT	1991	Re-registered 2001: GLZ 6555
1991	H621 FUT	" "	" " "	C49FT	1991	Re-registered 2001: GLZ 6557
1991	H623 FUT	" "	" " "	C49FT	1991	Re-registered 2001: GLZ 6556
1992	J405 AWF	" "	" " "	C49FT	1992	Re-registered 2001: ECZ 9144
1992	J406 AWF	" "	" " "	C49FT	1992	
1992	J407 AWF	" "	" " "	C49FT	1992	Re-registered 2001: ECZ 9145
1992	K713 RNR	Toyota Coaster	Caetano Optimo II	C18F	1992	
1992	K714 RNR	" "	" "	C18F	1992	
1993	K296 GDT	Bova 12-290	Bova Futura FHD	C49FT	1993	
1993	K297 GDT	" "	" " "	C49FT	1993	
1993	K298 GDT	" "	" " "	C49FT	1993	
1993	K299 GDT	" "	" " "	C49FT	1993	
1994	L405 LHE	Scania K113CLB	Irizar Century 12.35	C49FT	1994	
1994	L406 LHE	" "	" " "	C49FT	1994	
1994	L407 LHE	" "	" " "	C49FT	1994	
1994	L408 LHE	" "	" " "	C49FT	1994	
1995	M316 VET	" "	" " "	C49FT	1995	
1995	M317 VET	" "	" " "	C49FT	1995	
1995	M318 VET	" "	" " "	C49FT	1995	
1995	M319 VET	" "	" " "	C49FT	1995	
1996	N811 DKU	" "	" " "	C49FT	1996	
1996	N812 DKU	" "	" " "	C49FT	1996	
1996	N813 DKU	" "	" " "	C49FT	1996	
1996	N814 DKU	" "	" " "	C49FT	1996	
1996	N815 DKU	" "	" " "	C49FT	1996	
1997	P148 GHE	" "	" " "	C49FT	1997	
1997	P149 GHE	" "	" " "	C49FT	1997	
1998	R633 VNN	M.A.N. 18.310	Noge Catalan 350	C49FT	1998	
1998	R637 VNN	" "	" " "	C49FT	1998	
1998	R645 VNN	" "	" " "	C49FT	1998	
1999	T193 SUT	" "	" " "	C49FT	1999	
1999	T194 SUT	" "	" " "	C49FT	1999	
2000	V359 POB	Toyota Coaster	Caetano Optimo III	C22F	2000	
2000	W822 BOM	" "	" "	C22F	2000	
2000	W751 AAY	M.A.N. 18.350	Marcopolo Continental 340	C49FT	2000	
2000	W752 AAY	" "	" " "	C49FT	2000	
2002	FN02 HGG	M.A.N. 18.310	Noge Catalan 350	C49FT	2002	
2002	FN02 HGJ	" "	" " "	C49FT	2002	
2002	FN02 HGK	" "	" " "	C49FT	2002	
2002	FN02 HGM	" "	" " "	C49FT	2002	

Notes
(AD) Originally licensed to Arnold's Coaches but with Bowen fleet name
(a) EON 854 – original registration: AGX 829
(b) FON 855 – original registration: GN 8860
(c) FON 881 – original registration: ENE 693
(d) KJN 299 – original registration: ODS 465Y
(e) 12 DLY – original registration: HGA 830T
(f) 9712 WX – original registration: HGA 831T
(g) NFS 314T – later re-registered as: EOI 4363
(h) NFS 373T – later re-registered as: EOI 4364

Full details of the vehicles operated from the London (East Grinstead) base are not known but the following, from the main fleet, are known to have been based there at some time: YOX 506T, YOX 507T, EUK 548V, EUK 549V, GOV 573W. Two other coaches are known which were not from, and did not return to, the main fleet – TGD 991R an ex Park's of Hamilton Volvo B58 – Plaxton and RHP 8R a Volvo B58 – Caetano originally new to Supreme, Coventry but believed to have been acquired ex-Aston's, Kempsey.

L F BOWEN - Fleet List

L F BOWEN (FLIGHTS COACHES) LTD

Year Acquired	Reg No.	Chassis	Bodywork	Seats	Year New	Notes
1973	BNW 627C	AEC Reliance 2U3RA	Plaxton Panorama I	C51F	1965	Ex Flight's Tours Ltd
1973	FOP 701D	" " "	" " "	C45F	1966	" " " "
1973	FOP 702D	" " "	" " "	C37F	1966	" " " "
1973	ROE 704G	AEC Reliance 6U3ZR	Plaxton Panorama Elite	C49F	1969	" " " "
1973	ROE 705G	" " "	" " " "	C49F	1969	" " " "
1973	UOM 707H	" " "	" " " "	C55F	1970	" " " "
1973	UOM 708H	" " "	" " " "	C51F	1970	" " " "
1973	UOM 709H	" " "	" " " "	C51F	1970	" " " "
1970	YOB 710J	AEC Reliance 2U3RA	Plaxton Panorama Elite II	C53F	1971	" " " "
1973	YOB 720J	AEC Reliance 6U3ZR	Plaxton Panorama Elite II	C57F	1971	" " " "
1973	YOB 730J	" " "	" " " "	C57F	1971	" " " "
1973	YOB 740J	" " "	" " " "	C51F	1971	" " " "
1973	CVP 750K	" " "	" " " "	C57F	1972	" " " "
1973	CVP 770K	" " "	" " " "	C57F	1972	" " " "
1975	LOA 173P	Ford R1114	Duple Dominant	C53F	1975	
1975	LOA 174P	" "	" " "	C53F	1975	
1975	LOA 175P	" "	" " "	C53F	1975	
1975	LOA 176P	" "	" " "	C53F	1975	
1976	MOC 24P	" "	" " "	C53F	1976	

Notes:
The chassis of YOB 71OJ was originally from Flight's 717 MOB, new in 1964 with a Plaxton Panorama 37-seat body.
All of the 1975 and 1976 Fords were licensed to L F Bowen (Flights Coaches) Ltd but had L F Bowen fleet name and cream and maroon livery.

....

L F BOWEN (GLIDERWAYS) LTD

Year Acquired	Reg No.	Chassis	Bodywork	Seats	Year New	Notes
1973	UOH 635H	AEC Reliance	Caetano Lisboa	C51F	1970	Ex Bowen, Birmingham
1973	XOH 70J	Ford R226	Caetano Estoril	C53F	1971	" " " "
1973	XOH 71J	" "	" " "	C53F	1971	" " " "
1973	XOH 72J	" "	" " "	C53F	1971	" " " "
1973	XOH 73J	" "	" " "	C53F	1971	" " " "
1973	AOM 14K	" "	" " "	C53F	1971	" " " "
1973	AOM 15K	" "	" " "	C53F	1971	" " " "
1973	AOM 16K	" "	" " "	C53F	1971	" " " "
1973	AOM 17K	" "	" " "	C53F	1971	" " " "
1973	GOK 957L	Bedford YRT	Caetano Estoril II	C53F	1973	
1973	GOK 958L	" "	" " "	C53F	1973	
1973	HOM 472L	" "	" " "	C53F	1973	
1973	HOM 473L	" "	" " "	C53F	1973	
1975	JOH 948N	" "	" " "	C53F	1975	
1975	JOH 949N	" "	" " "	C53F	1975	
1975	JOH 950N	" "	" " "	C53F	1975	
1975	JOH 951N	" "	" " "	C53F	1975	
1976	MOC 19P	Ford R1114	Caetano Estoril II	C53F	1976	
1976	MOC 20P	" "	" " "	C53F	1976	
1976	MOC 21P	" "	" " "	C53F	1976	
1976	MOC 22P	" "	" " "	C53F	1976	
1976	MOC 23P	" "	" " "	C53F	1976	

Notes:
All vehicles (except JOH 948 – 951N and MOC 19 – 23P) were operated in grey and maroon livery.
JOH 948 – 951N were white and red.
MOC 19 – 23P were cream and maroon – some of these vehicles also carried L F Bowen "Superior Continental" fleet names.

L F BOWEN T/A YORKS COACHES

Current fleet as at January 2004

Year Acquired	Reg No.	Fleet No.	Chassis	Bodywork	Seats	Year New	Name
	FJ 6154		Maudslay ML3	Northern Counties	B31F	1929	Ex.Exeter Corp No. 5
1986	KPR 698	96	Kassbohrer-Setra	Setra S215HR Rationale	C49FT	1986	HMS Campbletown
1986	405 MDV	97	" " "	" " "	C53F	1986	HMS Battleaxe
1986	TVY 659	98	" " "	" " "	C53F	1986	HM Beaver
1988	UFC 221	70	Volvo B10M	Plaxton Paramount III 3500	C53F	1988	HMS Torbay
1988	XHO 856	85	Kassbohrer-Setra	Setra S215HR Rationale	C53F	1988	HMS Trenchant
1988	FSV 305	86	" " "	" " "	C53F	1988	HMS Trafalgar
1991	VHM 847	88	Kassbohrer-Setra	Setra S215HD	C49FT	1989	HMS Ark Royal
1994	ESK 897	53	Volvo B10M	Van-Hool Alizee	C53F	1988	HMS Sovereign
1995	XVY 392	54	Volvo B10M	Plaxton Paramount II 3200	C53F	1985	HMS Cumberland
1995	LUI 7871	55	Volvo B10M	Plaxton Paramount III 3200	C53F	1988	HMS Cornwall
1995	M116 MBD	16	Leyland-DAF	Deansgate	16	1995	HMS Spey
1996	HSK 511	90	Volvo B10M	Van-Hool Alizee	C49FT	1990	HMS Somerset
1996	846 FHA	92	Kassbohrer-Setra	Setra S215HD	C49FT	1993	HMS Iron Duke
1997	P117 ORP	17	Leyland-Daf	Coachliners	16	1997	HMS Cromer
1988	LUI 1525	71	M.A.N. 18.310	Noge Catalan 350	C49FT	1998	HMS Vengence
1988	ESK 896	72	" " "	" " "	C49FT	1998	HMS Vanguard
1998	XEA 745	73	" " "	" " "	C49FT	1998	HMS Vigilant
1999	T191 SUT	74	" " "	" " "	C49FT	1999	HMS Victorious
1999	T192 SUT	75	" " "	" " "	C49FT	1999	HMS Splendid
1999	T193 SUT	99	M.A.N. 24.400	Marcopolo Continental 360	C49FT	1999	HMS Ocean
2000	W751 AAY	94	" " "	" " "	C49FT	1999	HMS Invincible
2000	LUI 1503	696	Bova 12.290	Bova Futura FHD 12.35	C49FT	1988	HMS Fearless
2000	YJI 6038	18	Toyota Coaster	Caetano Optimo II	C18F	1992	HMS Penzance
2000	YJI 8597	19	" " "	" " "	C18F	1992	HMS Pembroke
2000	S604 VAY	93	M.A.N. 24.400	Noge Catalan 3.70	C49FT	1998	Chief
2001	Y664 NAY	91	M.A.N. 24.400	Marcopolo Continental 360	C49FT	2001	HMS Bulwark
2002	SYK 901	100	Neoplan N316SHD	Neoplan Cityliner	C48FT	1996	HMS Albion
2002	FN02 HGY	56	Dennis Javelin GX	Marcopolo Continental 340	C48FT	2002	HMS Grafton
2002	FN02 HGX	57	" " "	" " "	C48FT	2002	HMS Argyll
2002	FN02 HGU	58	" " "	" " "	C48FT	2002	HMS Kent
2003	MUI 1393	297	Bova 12.290	Bova Futura FHD 12.35	C49FT	1993	HMS Birmingham

Former registrations and owners…

ESK 897: E655 UNE, LSK 839, E619 CDS – Ex Park's, Hamilton
KPR 698: C96 LVV
TVY 659: C98 LVV
XHO 856: E85 LVV
VHM 847: F992 MTW – Ex Ball, Felixstowe
HSK 511: G880 VNA, WSV 528, G791 YND – Ex Shearing's
LUI 1525: R636 VNN
XEA 745: R638 VNN
YJI 6038: K713 RNR – Ex Bowen, Birmingham
SYK 901: N566 AWJ – Ex Bowen, Birmingham

XVY 392: B711 PEC, LIB 3766, B196 MAO – Ex Stainton, Kendal
405 MDV: C97 LVV
UFC 221: E70 LVV
FSV 305: E86 LVV
LUI 7871: XEA 745, E607 VNW, A20 MCW – Ex Wray, Harrogate
846 FHA: K121 OCT – Ex Spirit of London
ESK 896: R634 VNN
LUI 1503: F696 ONR – Ex Bowen, Birmingham
YJI 8597: K714 RNR – Ex Bowen, Birmingham
MUI 1393: K297 GDT – Ex Bowen, Birmingham

....

L. F. BOWEN T/A APPLEBYS COACH TRAVEL
Current fleet list as at January 2004

Year Acquired	Reg No.	Chassis	Bodywork	Seats	Year New
1996	N539 OFE	Scania K113CRB	Irizar Century 12.35	C49FT	1996
1996	N135 OFW	" " "	" " "	C49FT	1996
1996	N734 RBE	Scania K113TRB	Irizar Century 12.37	C49FT	1996
1996	N356 REE	" " "	" " "	C49FT	1996
1997	P388 WVL	" " "	" " "	C49FT	1997
1998	P 75 UJV	" " "	" " "	C49FT	1998
1998	R253 EJV	" " "	" " "	C49FT	1998
1998	R862 MFE	Scania K113CRB	Irizar Century 12.35	C49FT	1998
1998	R863 MFE	Scania K113TRB	Irizar Century 12.37	C49FT	1998
1999	T486 JJV	Scania K124IB6	Irizar Century 12.37	C49FT	1999
1999	T814 RTL	Scania K124IB4	Irizar Century 12.35	C49FT	1999
1999	T849 JFU	" " "	" " "	C49FT	1999
2000	W799 KVL	" " "	" " "	C49FT	2000
2000	W816 XEE	" " "	" " "	C49FT	2000

All vehicles acquired with the Appleby's Super Coach Holidays business in 2000

Arnold's Coaches, Tamworth

John Arnold (known as "Jack") started his business in the early 1920's when, at the age of 18 he set-up a taxi firm in the Dosthill area of Tamworth. In the early days Jack's brother, Herbert assisted with driving the cars and later John's wife, Gertie joined the business helping with the administration and cleaning of the vehicles.

Jack Arnold, driver Jack Shakespeare and Herbert Arnold. Tamworth Castle Museum

In 1926 Jack Arnold bought his first coach, a 14-seat Reo, which he operated under the name of "The Royal Blue". Two more Reos were purchased in 1928, one a 20-seater and the other with seats for 26 passengers.

He built up the firm at a depot known as "The Garage" on the Dosthill Road at Two Gates. Subsequent years saw more and more coaches acquired and the name of Arnold's Coaches became well known throughout the Tamworth area and the north of Birmingham. Although various makes were operated, Santus bodied Dennis Lancets – similar to those operated by L F Bowen – formed the main part of the fleet in the late

UE 5664 is a Reo Pullman 26-seater dating from 1928. Tamworth Castle Museum

Jack Arnold is pictured with UE 1003, one of his first coaches – an 8-seat Reo dating from 1926. Tamworth Castle Museum

1940's. The original fleet livery was cream and blue and Bedford chassis later became the usual choice for new purchases, although several used AECs also joined the fleet.

John Arnold died in 1960 by which time he had bought many of the rival firms in the area including Hickson Brothers and Albert Limm. The company ran for a year following his death before it was taken-over by Les Bowen who had been a long time friend of the Arnold's.

Arnold's Coaches remained a separate company and continued to flourish under its new ownership. In 1971 it moved from Two Gates to a new, larger, depot on the Fazeley Road, which remained operational until June 2003.

The Arnold's operation was different to that of the Birmingham based parent company. Much of the work undertaken was local contracts, in particular a series of services that served the many coal pits in the Tamworth area. These services were registered which enabled vehicles to be purchased under the bus grant scheme. Bedford and Ford remained the choice for chassis with bodies by Duple, Plaxton and Caetano, the fleet livery was changed to cream and maroon to match that of the parent company. Six unusual vehicles purchased in 1968 were a batch of Bedford VAM70 with dual-purpose Strachan bodies. It was also usual for vehicles to be transferred to Tamworth after seeing service in the Birmingham fleet.

The Arnold's name remained in use until the late 1970's although some coaches remained licensed to Arnolds Coaches but were operated in Bowen's livery.

A picture from the 1930's – the vehicle is a Gilford, possibly WD 1282 of 1930. The driver is Stanley Mayer, whose wife, Margaret can be seen in the open window with Mrs John Arnold beside her on the right.
Tamworth Castle Museum

FAC 527, one of two Duple Vista bodied Bedford OB's acquired by Arnold's in 1946.
Tamworth Castle Museum

Maudslay Marathon, HNX 768 from 1949 heads-up six Arnold's Coaches – all are Maudslays with Santus bodies. *Tamworth Castle Museum*

Another view of Arnold's Maudslays, from left to right; HAC 551 (1948), HWD 56 (1949), HNX 768 (1949), GNX 317 (1947), GWD 513 (1948), GUE 434 (1948) and HAC 550 (1949).
Tamworth Castle Museum

A Pictorial History of the Bowen Coach Group

Arnold's HAC 551, a 1948 Maudslay Marathon 3 with 33-seat Santus body.
R H G Simpson

Another Santus bodied Maudslay Marathon – HWD 56 was new to Arnold's in 1949.
R H G Simpson

Arnold's YUE 163 is a 1958 Bedford SB3 with 41-seat Plaxton Consort body.
R H G Simpson

A young Les Staley is pictured in front of YUE 163 – Les is now a Bowen's driver!

143

ARNOLD'S COACHES, TAMWORTH - Fleet List

Year Acquired	Reg No	Chassis	Bodywork	Seats	Year New	Notes
1924	NX 5813	Ford		B8	1924	
1926	UE 1003	Reo		B20	1926	
1928	UE 5644	"		B26	1928	
1928	UE 6525	"		B20	1928	
1928	VO 652	Gilford 168OT		B32	?	Ex Bowen, Birmingham
1930	WD 1282	" "		C32	1930	
1932	UT 9560	Maudslay ML3E	Willowbrook	B32F	1931	Ex Bircher, Ibstock
1934	WD 8013	Dennis Lancet	Willowbrook	C32F	1934	
1936	AWD 490	" "	" "	C32F	1936	
1937	BUE 746	Bedford WTB	Duple	C26F	1937	
1938	JD 144	Gilford 1665D	Wycombe	C32F	1930	Ex Fleet, Ilford
1943	EAC 122	Bedford OWB	Roe	B32F	1943	
1946	EWD 229	Bedford OB	Duple	C29F	1946	
1946	FAC 527	" "	"	C29F	1946	
1947	GNX 317	Maudslay Marathon III	Santus	C33F	1947	
1948	GUE 434	" "	"	C33F	1948	
1948	GWD 513	" "	"	C33F	1948	
1948	HAC 550	" "	"	C33F	1948	
1948	HAC 551	" "	"	C33F	1948	
1949	HNX 768	" "	"	C33F	1949	
1949	HWD 56	" "	"	C33F	1949	
1954	HOM 917	" "	"	C33F	1948	Ex Bowen, Birmingham
1955	PRF 862	Leyland PS1/1	Bellhouse Hartwell	C35F	1948	Ex Hickson Bros., Tamworth
1955	LHA 321	Leyland PS1/1	Duple	C33F	1948	" " " "
1955	RRE 121	Maudslay Marathon	Santus	C33F	1948	" " " "
1956	UAC 99	Bedford SBG	Yeates	C41F	1956	
1956	UNX 425	" "	"	C41F	1956	
1957	WNX 109	Bedford SB3	Plaxton Consort	C41F	1957	
1957	WNX 110	" "	" "	C41F	1957	
1958	YNX 371	" "	" "	C41F	1958	
1958	YUE 163	" "	" "	C41F	1958	
1959	NAH 279	Bedford SB	Duple Vega	C33F	1952	Ex Babbage, Cromer
1960	GBA 108	" "	" "	C37F	1953	Ex Parkin, Borrowash
1960	SEA 780	Bedford SB3	Duple Vega	C41F	1958	Ex Hill, West Bromwich
1960	XNG 500	" "	" "	C41F	?	Ex Babbage, Cromer
1960	TOC 526	Bedford SBG	Yeates	C41F	?	Ex James, Birmingham
1960	FSN 119	Bedford SBG	Plaxton	C41F	?	Ex Garlochhead Coach Service
1961	RYV 439	Bedford SBG	Duple	C41F	?	Ex Gray, Grendon Underwood
1961	YUT 419	Bedford CALV	Martin Walter	B11	1961	
1962	8837 WD	Bedford SB5	Burlingham Seagull	C41F	1962	
1962	8838 WD	" "	" "	C41F	1962	
1963	898 LTE	Bedford SB1	Plaxton	C41F	?	Ex Wall, Wigan
1963	899 LTE	" "	"	C41F	?	"
1963	6706 WE	Bedford SB3	Plaxton	C41F	1959	Ex Hirst & Sweeting, Sheffield
1963	HOR 474	Dennis Lancet III	Duple	C33F	?	Ex Budden, West Tytherley
1963	FBN 100	AEC Regal IV	Burlingham	C41C	?	Ex Williams, Glasgow
1963	MXB 468	AEC Regal IV	Duple	C41C	1952	Ex Timpson, London
1963	MXB 469	" "	" "	C41C	1952	" " "
1963	140 JAC	Bedford SB5	Plaxton Embassy	C41F	1963	
1963	141 JAC	" "	" "	C41F	1963	
1963	142 JAC	" "	" "	C41F	1963	
1964	500 EHO	AEC Reliance	Burlingham	C51F	1962	Ex Creamline, Bordon
1964	FXT 283	AEC Regent	LPTB	H56RD	?	Ex Smith, Reading
1965	111 CPB	AEC Reliance	Yeates	C41F	?	Ex Richmond, Epsom
1965	CWD 707C	Bedford SB5	Harrington Crusader	C41F	1965	
1965	CWD 708C	" "	" "	C41F	1965	
1965	CWD 709C	" "	"	C41F	1965	
1965	HNR 275	Bedford SB	Plaxton	C37F	1952	Ex Whitcombe, Tamworth
1965	796 COE	Bedford SB8	Harrington Crusader	C41F	1961	Ex Bowen, Birmingham
1965	797 COE	" "	" "	C41F	1961	" " " "
1965	794 JOB	AEC Reliance	Plaxton Panorama	C49F	1963	" " " "
1965	SOB 49	Daimler	Duple	C41C	1953	Ex Newton, Birmingham
1965	MOK 711	Leyland PSU1	Willowbrook	C37C	1952	" " " "
1965	5261 PH	Bedford CALV	Martin Walter	11	1963	Ex Bowser, Westerham
1966	PBF 931D	Bedford VAM14	Strachan	DP45F	1966	
1966	PBF 932D	" "	"	DP45F	1966	
1966	PBF 933D	" "	"	DP45F	1966	
1966	PBF 934D	" "	"	DP45F	1966	
1966	PBF 935D	" "	"	DP45F	1966	
1966	PBF 936D	" "	"	DP45F	1966	
1966	301 NOF	Bedford VAL14	Plaxton Panorama	2F	1964	Ex Newton, Birmingham
1967	100 HOR	Bedford VAL14	Duple Vega Major	C52F	?	Ex Cole, Eastbourne
1967	901 KHO	" "	" "	C52F	?	Ex Weeks, Sutton Valence
1967	FAA 435D	" "	" "	C52F	1966	Ex Elme Park, Romford
1967	EOT 721D	Bedford VAL14	Plaxton Panorama	C52F	1966	Ex Queens Park, Croydon

ARNOLD'S COACHES, TAMWORTH - Fleet List

Year Acquired	Reg No	Chassis	Bodywork	Seats	Year New	Notes
1967	EVP 689D	Ford R192	Duple	C45F	1966	Ex Eatonways, Birmingham
1967	EVP 691D	" "	"	C45F	1966	" " " "
1967	EVP 692D	" "	"	C45F	1966	" " " "
1967	EVP 693D	" "	"	C45F	1966	" " " "
1968	NRE 289F	Bedford VAM70	Duple Viceroy	C45F	1968	
1968	NRE 290F	" "	" "	C45F	1968	
1968	NRE 291F	" "	" "	C45F	1968	
1968	NRE 292F	" "	" "	C45F	1968	
1968	ORF 483F	Bedford VAM70	Plaxton Panorama I	C45F	1968	
1968	ORF 484F	" "	" "	C45F	1968	
1970	JAA 498E	Bedford VAL14	Duple Viceroy	C52F	1967	Ex Hodge, Sandhurst
1970	SBJ 813F	Bedford VAL70	Duple (Northern)	C52F	1968	Ex Braybridge, Mendlesham
1971	XBF 328J	Ford R226	Caetano Estoril	C53F	1971	
1971	XBF 329J	" "	" "	C53F	1971	
1971	NUX 111G	Bedford VAM70	Duple Viceroy	C45F	1969	Ex Whittle, Highley
1971	NNM 482H	Ford Transit	LCM	12	1970	Ex Huntley, Luton
1971	ERF 207K	Bedford YRQ	Duple Viceroy	C45F	1971	
1973	GOE 832L	Bedford YRT	Caetano Estoril II	C53F	1973	
1973	GOE 833L	" "	" "	C53F	1973	
1973	GOE 834L	" "	" "	C53F	1973	
1973	GOE 835L	" "	" "	C53F	1973	
1974	YOH 21J	Bedford YRQ	Duple Viceroy	C45F	1971	Ex Bowen, Birmingham
1974	YOH 22J	" "	" "	C45F	1971	" " " "
1974	YOH 227J	" "	" "	C45F	1971	" " " "
1974	YOA 693J	" "	" "	C45F	1971	" " " "
1974	YOA 694J	" "	" "	C45F	1971	" " " "
1974	YOH 849J	" "	" "	C45F	1971	" " " "
1974	YOH 850J	" "	" "	C45F	1971	" " " "
1974	COG 32K	Bedford YRQ	Caetano Cascais	C45F	1972	" " " "
1974	COG 34K	" "	" "	C45F	1972	" " " "
1974	COG 35K	" "	" "	C45F	1972	" " " "
1974	COG 36K	" "	" "	C45F	1972	" " " "
1974	COG 37K	" "	" "	C45F	1972	" " " "
1974	COG 38K	" "	" "	C45F	1972	" " " "
1974	CON 281K	" "	" "	C45F	1972	" " " "
1974	CON 282K	" "	" "	C45F	1972	" " " "
1974	DRF 118N	Bedford YRT	Plaxton Elite III Express	C53F	1974	
1974	DRF 119N	" "	" " "	C53F	1974	
1974	DRF 120N	" "	" " "	C53F	1974	
1974	DRF 121N	" "	" " "	C53F	1974	
1975	KVP 938P	Ford R1114	Duple Dominant	C53F	1975	
1975	KVP 939P	" "	" "	C53F	1975	
1975	KVP 940P	" "	" "	C53F	1975	
1975	KVP 941P	" "	" "	C53F	1975	
1975	KVP 942P	" "	" "	C53F	1975	
1975	KVP 943P	" "	" "	C53F	1975	
1975	KVP 944P	" "	" "	C53F	1975	
1975	KVP 945P	" "	" "	C53F	1975	

Although further vehicles were licensed to Arnold's they carried Bowens fleet name and are therefore included in the Bowen's fleet list from 1976 onwards.